MILLION DOLLAR TRAP

Step-By-Step Business Plan to Scale Beyond the 7-Figure Plateau

BY TRACY COUSINEAU

Million Dollar Trap

By Tracy Cousineau

This work is exclusively published and facilitated by Beverly Hills Publishing
468 Camden Drive, Beverly Hills, CA 90210
www.beverlyhillspublishing.com

Copyright © 2021, Tracy Cousineau. All rights reserved.
ISBN: 978-1-7360900-5-3

In no way is it legal to reproduce, duplicate, or transmit any part of this document in either electronic means or in printed format. Recording of this publication is strictly prohibited and any storage of this document is not allowed unless with written permission from the publisher. All rights reserved.

The information provided herein is stated to be truthful and consistent, in that any liability, in terms of inattention or otherwise, by any usage or abuse of any policies, processes, or directions contained within is the solitary and utter responsibility of the recipient reader. Under no circumstances will any legal responsibility or blame be held against the publisher for any reparation, damages, or monetary loss due to the information herein, either directly or indirectly. Respective authors own all copyrights not held by the publisher. The information herein is offered for informational purposes solely and is universal, as so. The presentation of the information is without contract or any type of guarantee assurance.

The trademarks that are used are without any consent, and the publication of the trademark is without permission or backing by the trademark owner. All trademarks and brands within this book are for clarifying purposes only and are owned by the owners themselves, not affiliated with this document.

The information and descriptions presented in this book and in Million Dollar Trap newsletters and website are intended for adults, age 18 and over, and are solely for informational and educational purposes. Tracy Cousineau does not give legal, psychological, or financial advice. Before beginning any new business or personal development routine, or if you have specific legal, psychological, or medical concerns, a medical, financial, legal, or other professional should be consulted.

Any reproduction, republication, or other distribution of this work, including, without limitation, the duplication, copying, scanning, uploading, and making available via the internet or any other means, without the express permission of the publisher is illegal and punishable by law, and the knowing acquisition of an unauthorized reproduction of this work may subject the acquirer to liability. Please purchase only authorized electronic or print editions of this work and do not participate in or encourage electronic piracy of copyrighted materials. Your support of the author's rights is appreciated.

This document is geared towards providing exact and reliable information with regards to the topic and issue covered. The publication is sold with the idea that the publisher is not required to render accounting, officially permitted, or otherwise, qualified services. If advice is necessary, legal or professional, a practiced individual in the profession should be ordered.

– From a Declaration of Principles which was accepted and approved equally by a Committee of the American Bar Association and a Committee of Publishers and Associations.

Thank you to everyone that sat back and allowed me to fail, to the ones who said I wouldn't make it, and especially to the unsupportive haters who allowed me to feed from their energy to be an unstoppable and unbreakable champion.

To my beautiful daughters who I will never leave standing alone.

To Neil, my ~~Adopted~~ Dad, YOU taught me more lessons on strength and independence than you will ever know.

And to my amazing publisher and Adderall who never left my side, without them both, you wouldn't be reading this.

TABLE OF CONTENTS

Introduction: Where You Come From Does Not Make You Who You Are 1

Chapter 1:

An Unexpected Success Story 5

Chapter 2:

Get Out Of Your Own Head. 21

Chapter 3:

Beyond Your Million Dollar Brand 41

Chapter 4:

You Are Your Own Competition 63

Chapter 5:

From Burnout to Beach Mode 79

Chapter 6:
Uplevel Your Inner Circle 93

Chapter 7:
Quit Yourself 105

Chapter 8:
The Growth Zone 113

Chapter 9:
Celebrate...119

INTRODUCTION: WHERE YOU COME FROM DOES NOT MAKE YOU WHO YOU ARE

If there's one thing I've learned, it's that we all have the power to carve our own path in life, no matter what limitations are set upon us. I always knew I had this power within me, but I struggled with my identity for most of my life. I was raised in an environment of bullying, addiction, and betrayal.

Yet despite all odds, I've built and co-built several multimillion dollar businesses, and have found true joy and passion in coaching other women to break through their limiting mindsets.

Have you ever seen the Statue of Liberty? I remember the first time I did. It gave off this power and energy that made me proclaim to myself and to the world, "Damn, I'm going to stand up tall. I'm going to stand up with my right arm and my left arm out. I'm going to hold my torch, and I'm going to run with it. I'm going to take that Statue of Liberty stance." Her image has been a guiding light as I've followed my path to building multiple seven-figure businesses – and beyond.

When you're in business, getting to that first million takes grit and hustle. And while this "hustle mentality" can give you endurance in the beginning, it will ultimately be your downfall. You see, the hustle is addictive. Like any drug, it gives you a burst of energy and a false belief that you have more confidence than you truly have deep down in your core. I've seen many badass female business owners get attached to their hustle, and I've been one of them.

If you aren't willing to let go of that hustle, then you'll never move beyond the million dollar mark. Because at that million dollar hustle mentality, you're just waking up every day and you're doing the same thing over and over again. You wake up in a state of anxiety, and you cling to whatever client or opportunity comes your way. You lower your standards for who you let "in," and you ultimately end up exhausting your energy and time on difficult people and situations. You run on burnout mode, where you know you're not showing up to your potential, but you're showing up just enough to maintain your million. You've fallen into what I call *The Million Dollar Trap*.

You need to break that cycle of thinking so that you can move beyond that reality and grow from your multimillion dollar foundation.

Once you stop hustling and look beyond to the next level that your dream is calling you to go, you'll realize that the secret is having the right tribe, the right people around you, and listening *only* to that inner voice that says, "You can." You may be wondering where you find all these uplifting people or how you get the unstoppable mindset, and we are going to be diving deep into all of this later in the book. Let me give you a sneak peek at one of the secrets you will soon discover: having the right people around you comes from having the right energy. Become open to the idea that you might have to make some changes in order to break out of the hustle trap, especially when it comes to the environments you're in.

I've learned that making changes in your life is a step-at-a-time process. But once you get past step 10, somewhere around step 15, you'll realize, "Crap, I'm running now!" You're no longer walking, you're sprinting in your stilettos, because you're seeing that you can get through the shit – and the faster you get through the shit, the bigger opportunities come in a better way and even faster than you could ever imagine possible.

When you tap into that energy of boldly walking each step of your path, your outcome, your aura, everything just switches on. You can just see it. *It's your light.*

When you stand in your light, you're not only able to overcome the limitations of your past, you're able to avoid falling into the million dollar trap.

Now, kick back, because I'm going to take you on a trip to the past. May you find inspiration in my story of how I pulled myself up from the bottom rungs, and may you too realize that where you came from does not make you *who* you are.

CHAPTER 1:
AN UNEXPECTED SUCCESS STORY

Do you know what I love about doing business today? I love that anyone – no matter what their background, environment, sex, religion, sexual affiliation, or demographic – can create a business and a brand built by their dreams.

The tools we have today have skyrocketed opportunities for people who want to be their own boss and create value for others to find the exact audience who will appreciate what they have to offer. It truly is a whole new world for entrepreneurialism, and I am constantly amazed at what is possible with today's technology. But back when I first started in business, it wasn't that way.

I was, to put it frankly, a hyperactive military brat with an addictive personality, who was simultaneously super introverted and kept to myself.

I graduated high school early because I was bored. I had severe ADHD, but that diagnosis wasn't around back in the day, and the adults around me just thought I couldn't comprehend information. The truth was that I assimilate information very quickly, and the pace at which I was learning in school was boring to me. I just wanted to daydream and tune out.

I was getting by with Cs and Ds, and I just felt like I sucked. I'd hear my friends say they drank coffee and stayed up studying for exams, and I'd do the same, but I'd show up and fail – the caffeine burned me out and I couldn't stay awake.

Later in life, I realized that I learned differently than I was being trained to learn in school. I have a photographic memory, and I retain information through images and different colors. I was blessed to have ADHD. I just didn't understand it. Nobody understood it then, but once I learned about it, I was able to grow from it. When doctors wanted to start giving me medicine, I said, "Oh no, no, my brain works a certain way. And now that I understand how it works, I'm getting a lot out of it." This was a major piece of what got me to where I am. I took other people's predictions of, "Oh, you'll never make it because you're just C and D kind of girl," to, "Heck, no, I'm an entrepreneur with a clear vision. Watch me do this."

When I started recognizing my unique power of learning, I knew that I didn't want to be in school anymore. I decided to go to summer school and vocational school and picked up more credits so I could graduate sooner. Once I graduated at age 17, I started working three jobs, building my experience. Fast forward 11 years later, I decided I couldn't work in corporate America anymore. I felt like working for other people wasn't what I wanted to do. I wanted to be able to have my own businesses, and not clocking in from 9:00 to 5:00. That became my goal.

And that's when I started real estate at age 28.

Just before I discovered that path, I was in property management, and it dawned on me that if I could make $80,000 leasing apartments, selling houses should be pretty darn easy.

At that time, I also had an experience with a tenant that pushed me over the edge. They had done a lot of damage to a brand new community in the middle of the night and started calling me collect from jail. I was getting dragged into their divorce, and it was extremely stressful. At that point, I knew it was time to move on from my job and corporate America.

Every night, I would drive by this community college on the way home and would be drawn to a red flashing sign advertising a real estate course. I decided to look into it, and then I signed up. I got my real estate license within about a two-and-a-half-month period. I had $12,000 in my 401(k). So I got the money out of the 401(k) and put it directly into beginning my real estate career.

MY FIRST REAL ESTATE DEAL

I remember making my first deal. While I was still in real estate school, I knew the only company that I wanted to work for was the one with the hot-air balloon. At the time, this brokerage didn't hire new agents. I remember reaching out to the broker at a local office and he wouldn't even take my call. I had no experience. Without experience, I was not worth the call.

We went around class one night and were asked, "Where are you going to work?" Everyone was naming these mom and pop companies, and I mentioned the hot-air balloon brokerage. They all started chuckling at me, like, "This girl has no idea what she's talking about. They won't hire her straight out of school." At this stage in my life, I was humiliated and beet red. That shy introvert was determined to change the outcome!

That class was on a Tuesday. I would have been back at school on Thursday, but I was like, "I'm going to prove these people wrong."

On Wednesday, I had a goal. I'd see the signs with the hot-air balloons everywhere, and I just knew that's what I wanted to identify myself with.

And so I called the broker's office again, and again until I got him on the phone. His name was Bill. I told him I wanted to work there. And he told me the same thing: they didn't hire new agents.

I tried to explain to him that he didn't know me, he didn't know my drive, and how could he allow those rules to stop somebody else's goals?

And he just said, "I'm sorry, it's just part of our policy." So I put a note on the door at the apartment community I was working at, and I decided to drive to his office.

I remember going into the office and telling Pamela, the receptionist, that I was there to see Bill. I remember her saying, "Is he expecting you?"

CHAPTER 1: AN UNEXPECTED SUCCESS STORY

"Nope," I said. "He's not expecting me."

She said, "Okay, well, he's in a meeting."

"Okay," I replied. "Well, I'll just wait right here on the couch for him."

I sat, and I waited, and he finally came out.

When he saw me, Bill immediately said, "We've already spoken. I let you know the process."

I said, "Just give me five minutes." I made a deal with Bill that I would pay the brokerage the upfront fee of $850, and if didn't sell my first house in 30 days I would leave. "You'll never see me again," I assured him. "I'll just go."

I was able to sell my first house in 10 days to a cash buyer. I still remember the exact ad and house to this day. And, of course, they never asked me to leave. After years in the business, I became one of the top agents in their office.

Don't let people – or policies – stop you from going for your vision and your goals. You never know what could happen as a result of your persistence and boldness.

It was amazing to me that everyone I talked to was so set on, "This is what the policy is. This is what the rule is," instead of saying, "Well, maybe we shouldn't have that. Maybe we should think of something different."

And guess what? They are different now. Those policies they had in the past have completely changed – now they hire everybody, regardless of experience.

Had I allowed that initial roadblock to determine my path, I don't know where I would be today. I just knew that was the path I wanted to take. I could feel it aligning for me, the more I stepped into my power and owned my vision.

Today, I own, operate and broker one of the fastest-growing privately owned real estate firms in America, founded an empowering women's group, and I own a clothing boutique. I guess you can say I've earned the title "business mogul."

Just like my classmates laughed when I announced who I'd work for, I've been constantly surrounded by all these voices that didn't take me seriously. As I grew and progressed through my personal challenges in life, I'd go through cycles of people observing me and saying, "Sure, she's making some changes, but she's going to revert back. She's doing that hustle to get through, but she won't see the other side because things are holding her back." The only person who ever truly had my back was myself – even from childhood.

Now, kick back and relax, 'cause we're about to do a little time traveling.

LIES AND ILLUSIONS

From a young age, I was living in lies and illusion. We grew up military, so you just didn't ask questions. You did what you were told to do.

We didn't have a large amount of money, and I was bullied a lot at school. I can remember kids saying to me, "Oh, those aren't the right shoes." Or, "Your Jordache jeans are actually the boys' version, not the girls' version." I know my parents provided the best they could, but at the time it just sucked.

CHAPTER 1 :: AN UNEXPECTED SUCCESS STORY

I didn't have the mental and emotional security that most people have growing up. There was a huge void I could feel, that I didn't understand. Something was not quite right in my family.

I remember bits and pieces of my childhood, of situations where my parents, usually my mom, would act really, really strange. But I couldn't figure it out. Some of our baby pictures, if you flipped them over, there'd be a name on the back that was crossed out. On some level, I was always wondering "What's going on? What don't I know?" But I was so young that I didn't have those thoughts consciously. I knew that not everything made sense, but when I would question myself about it, it made perfect sense. My older brother and sister looked like my dad who raised me, my brother and I looked like my mom, and my little sister looked like both of them. I had no real reason to question my parentage, but it turns out I was tuning in to the truth intuitively.

Later in life, after I'd moved out from my parents' house, I found out the father who raised me actually adopted me when I was 10.

Once I found that out, my mind went back to when I was 10, and I could remember some really weird things that were hard to explain.

One time, my grandmother came to stay with us for a week. My parents went somewhere, but they wouldn't tell us where they were going. Another time, a week after that, my brother and I were told that two of our siblings were taking a trip without the rest of us, and we didn't understand why.

We lived on a military base at the time, and my brother and I (we were eight or nine years old) were playing in the backyard. Suddenly we saw these lights flashing through our playroom, and we panicked. We thought our playroom was on fire. We started throwing rocks through the window – and then our older sister and brother popped out. All of us were confused. "Wait a minute. You're not supposed to be here. What happened?"

Little did we know that my parents were in a custody battle with my biological father, and they had been in court the time when my grandmother came to stay with us for a week. This time, my grandparents couldn't come and watch us, so they dealt us kids out to three different families. The lights we thought were a fire in the playroom was actually the TV playing. Later, we asked our parents why my brother and sister were in the house, but the story we got was never the truth. It was like, "Oh yeah, they got back earlier than we expected," or some other explanation.

These were the type of situations that sparked my fixation to dig deeper. In a way, I was addicted to knowing more. And that's just my personality. If I'm really into something, really, really passionate about it, I'm just going to keep asking or digging. That's what I do with work and in business.

On top of the secrecy in my family, there was also a lot of addiction.

My mom is passed now, and we were able to reconnect after our challenging times and I miss her dearly, but growing up, our relationship had all the qualities of the 1981 film "Mommie Dearest."

CHAPTER 1: AN UNEXPECTED SUCCESS STORY

She was against drinking because my real dad was an alcoholic. Her addiction was gambling, bingo, and shopping. She didn't work and she was always gone at night, playing bingo. She was also OCD. If she turned the light switch off once, she'd flip it 10 more times. Up and down, up and down, up and down. (The things I hated then, I miss so much now.)

I would come home sometimes to find everything in my closet and drawers thrown in the middle of my floor. I would spend hours having to refold and rehang things to meet her standards. On the weekends, every hairbrush was Comet cleaned, and we were scrubbing and doing massive chores. We just did it, because we sure didn't want to get the mouth soap, sentence writing, standing in the corner, or the dreaded spanking.

I would find myself, as I got older, trying to get attention from my parents by going along with their addictions and hobbies. We didn't grow up with the I love you's or the hugs or the kisses. With my dad, it was, "Let me go to the races with you, and sit in the stands with you, because I just want that time with you." Or with my mom, it was, "I'm going to go to a smoke-covered bingo hall and play bingo with my mom and act like I like it, just so that I can be next to her." That was the only sense of connection that I could get from them.

It's really sad to see how addiction has affected so many members of my family, and my friends. I look at where many of their lives have gone, and I see how horrible the outcome of any type of addiction can be. Some people can't break the cycle.

Unfortunately, my brother, my only true 100% sibling, is one of those people. He has been in and out of jail for having too many DUIs and domestic abuse.

What I realized is every time I thought that he had hit rock bottom, I was bailing him out. He was writing me these sappy letters from jail saying that he was going to get out and go work at a church and speak on his experience to help other people.

After one particular cycle of being in prison and getting out, he and his girlfriend were working at this church and living in some house that was full of mold. I felt really bad for them; they were in an unhealthy environment and didn't have a lot of money. At the time I was single with three children and needed to have some help myself. I decided to let him and his girlfriend, Carrie, live in my basement, which was newly remodeled.

No drinking was allowed in my house, no drugs, no nothing. And my brother appeared to adapt for the better. He'd get up every morning and read the Bible on the back porch. He helped with yard work, he and his girlfriend cooked, they took care of the household while I went and worked to pay all the bills.

The recession was starting to unfold about this time too. Because he'd been in and out of the system for so long, my brother realized that after 30 days, he had legal residency, and would have to be evicted. So day 31, he and his girlfriend went and got drunk on margaritas at a Mexican restaurant around the corner from my house. They came back to the house absolutely smashed, mean, and angry. He threatened to hurt me, telling me I was going to be chopped into 500 pieces, and no one would ever know, and that he saw a lot in prison and he doesn't have a problem going back.

So the next day I said, "You know what? This isn't going to work. I let you know that there are no drugs, no alcohol in my house, and I'm not having any of this. My kids are not going to be around this. I'm not going to be around this. You're going to have to leave."

My daughter, who's 25 now, was 15 years old at the time. She was in the kitchen while we were having this discussion, getting ready to go somewhere. She put her hand on my brother's – her uncle's – shoulder, to move him just a little bit so she could get around him in the kitchen. And he threw a cup of hot coffee into her face.

I called the police, and when they arrived my brother said, "No, she pushed me first."

The cop said, "Well, if he's going to claim that she put her hands on him and pushed him, he was defending himself. Your 15-year-old is going to have to go to jail, too." It was nuts.

I went to file their eviction, but his girlfriend came to me and she said, "I'm so scared of your brother. Can I stay here? My grandmother lives in Mississippi. Can I just watch the kids for a few weeks, make some money, and go take a bus to Mississippi?"

I believed her. I felt sorry for her, all that. I would say I used to be really, really gullible. They played me for a fool – and I learned from that, too.

What I didn't realize was that he and his girlfriend had something planned.

The day it happened, the kids were preparing for an open house at their school, and they were getting ready in my room. They told me that Carrie kept going back and forth from my room to my closet, and then downstairs to the basement. Well, what she was doing was filling up all of my suitcases with everything of value of mine in my house.

Later that day, I got a call from my neighbor.

"Don't freak out. I have your infant. I just moved in. This is the house I live in. You don't know me, but your brother and his girlfriend dropped her off at my house. Just get here when you can."

They had brought my five-week-old baby – who had just gotten out of NICU – over to the neighbor's house, while I was just getting back to work. They made up some crazy story about me and told the neighbor that they had to get away from me. They convinced her to drop them off at a local parking lot, and said, "Don't call her until you get back home so that we can get out of here."

When I got home, I saw that they'd taken everything out of my house that they could sell quickly. My computers, cameras, clothes, shoes, tools – anything that they could that would be sold to make some fast cash. And I never saw them again.

I put a criminal trespassing warrant against him, so he wasn't allowed to be anywhere around us. But when my mom was passing away, a few years after that, I knew I needed to let him know. I could tell that she was holding off from just peacefully going because she wanted to see him and say goodbye.

At that time, we were in the recession, and I only had a couple of hundred bucks. I reached out to him, and I said, "Look, I'll take my money and I will get you a flight. You just have to tell me where the closest airport or bus is. Come here and see mom so that she can peacefully go. She's in pain. I know she wants to see you and that's why she's holding on."

He was supposed to call me the next day to set everything up. And instead, he played the victim and decided that he was the one in pain, not mom. He went out and got drunk. He got in a fight with his girlfriend, pulled a knife on her, and ended up in jail.

Mom passed away two days later. And he didn't come to the funeral, nothing.

He tried to reach me around eight months ago, wanting to buy a house in Florida, but I am long done.

Sometimes, you have to hit some type of rock bottom in order to understand the effects that addiction has on your life. My brother is an example of someone who never did. You can't just tell somebody who's in an addictive cycle, "Oh, you should take that energy and put it to this," because they've not hit a discomfort level that will wake them up from the inside. Even my daughter has struggled with her addictions, and I had to be ready for her to hear the wake-up call on her own. I am so proud of her sobriety!

You could say, "Just go to AA and you can change," but you have to have the power from within yourself to do that. And unfortunately, some people don't understand that that power lies in their own mind. They allow something else to take power over them.

For me, I knew that I wasn't going to allow these cycles to continue in my life. I knew that I wasn't going to allow some chemical imbalance to control me. I just had to learn to control it.

I'm so grateful that I was able to break the cycle of my own addiction, and that I can put that energy fully into my work.

It is powerful to have an addiction – but you have to put the energy of it somewhere meaningful so that it does not ruin you.

OBSTACLES THAT MAKE YOU STRONGER

Earlier, I shared with you that I felt this void inside me as a child. Eventually, I realized that the emptiness I felt was this not-knowing, this discomfort with the people in my life who raised me and weren't honest about who they were – or who I was.

As I grew up and learned more about my mom, my adoptive father, and my real father, the void in me started to fill. At the same time, I got mad. I basically regressed into my child self, and I started acting out. I didn't care what anyone wanted from me or told me.

My attitude was, "Whatever. I'm going to go here, I'm going to do that." I didn't know what in my life wasn't a lie, and it hurt. I went through the cycle of denial, anger, and betrayal that happens when somebody you love passes away. As I grew up and had my own children, became an adult, and understood life better, I realized that maybe we shouldn't always hold grudges and that we can instead ask more questions to understand all sides of the story.

Needless to say, I faced a lot of obstacles early on in my life. I'm sure you have as well, in your own way. All of this happens for a reason, in my opinion. I know that without my experiences, I wouldn't be able to have empathy for people, much less coach them through starting their own businesses or purchasing a home.

I sell hundreds of homes and encounter hundreds of people a year, all over the place. How could I possibly help other people through their obstacles in life, if I've never been through them myself?

Have you ever received advice from a coach or a professional and walked away thinking, "Why would I take that advice? That makes no sense." I've sat back from experiences like that and realized that those coaches have never been through what I've been through. They might've picked their tools up from another coach, the internet, or a book, and that's why they say what they say, but they've never had boots on the ground.

For me, I don't feel good talking to people about things I haven't experienced. I wouldn't tell anybody to do something I haven't already done. I wouldn't advise anybody on what the outcome might be if I've never been through their situation. This is a big part of my philosophy as a leader, and it's why I wanted to share with you a little backstory on the environments that shaped me.

They say that your life is a reflection of the average of the five people you spend the most time with. Take a look at those five people in your life right now, and recognize that if you're not where you want to be in life, you can consider them your past tribe. You don't have to bail anyone out of jail. You don't need the care, approval, or attention of people who are trapped in their own cycles of addiction and seeking. Trust me – they're not going where you're going.

Trust that your passion will continue to grow. Your love for what you do is going to continue to grow. The right people will come and surround you. Know that your past doesn't define where you can go in the future.

I know now that if we're trapped in any negative cycles, the most valuable thing we can do is be open to the power of our minds to shape our destiny.

My hope for you is that this book will ignite a fire within you, that will allow you to accomplish so much in life, and to stop holding back.

Whether it's breaking out of a negative thought pattern or breaking through the ceiling of one million dollars in your business, you have everything you need inside you to succeed.

CHAPTER 2:
GET OUT OF YOUR OWN HEAD

People change and people learn from their lessons, and that's how you mature and that's how you grow. Life lessons are very important because they make you who you are, and they can make you stronger, they can make you wiser, and smarter. My past allowed me to really be who I needed to be in my life – a dominant, strong, and decisive businesswoman, who is also caring, sensitive, and nurturing of others.

These lessons also helped me stretch my mind and think differently. I believe that if everything had always been handed to me, I would've thought I was entitled to everything, and would never learn the value of anything. My hard knocks also helped me grow from being a very gullible introvert to having a bold personality and speaking my truth. I used to "cupcake" everything, skirting around important conversations, because I didn't have the heart to tell people what I was thinking. Now, whatever I'm thinking, you're going to know.

I also learned the value of tuning other people out and listening only to my inner voice. I remember people saying about me, "Oh, she'll never make it." "She'll never do this," or, "She'll never do that." And I used to let it get to me, let myself fall under that umbrella of, "Yup, you know what? I suck. If they say I can't do it, that means I can't do it."

Do you relate to this? How many times have you stopped yourself from going for your dreams because of what other people have said, or because of how they've hurt you in the past?

I had to go through that many times, to realize that if you can get through all the shit in your life without rain boots on, you can get through a lot of shit in heels.

When it comes to my brother, it's been 10 years. I had to go through the grieving process of letting him go, realizing that some people are put in our lives for seasons. He is family, and I don't ever wish any harm on him. But he's a grown adult, and he has to make his own choices in life, just like I do. And my choice is not to be around what he's bringing.

Ultimately, I want you to know that as a business leader, you have to let others in. You have to guide, you have to lead others, and let others help you grow. There's no way you can build a multiple seven-figure empire with hustle alone, thinking you can do it by yourself. You may get to six figures or multiple six figures, but you're never going to break that seven-figure, if you're not letting go of this belief that you have to do at all yourself.

CHAPTER 2:: GET OUT OF YOUR OWN HEAD

In this chapter, I'm going to share some of the important lessons I learned when it comes to trusting people to take the vision in your head and work with you to create it. We're going to talk about hiring, firing, delegating, and expanding your business outside of your own head, into the hands of a capable team.

PRACTICING DELEGATION

Practicing delegation is a major key to getting to the next level in your business.

Many business people have resistance to delegating. We all know the saying, "If you want it done right, do it yourself." Maybe you've even heard yourself thinking, "By the time that I train somebody to do this, I could have done it myself."

That was true for me for a long time. I always looked at everything as, "Why hire somebody if I can do it? I'll save that money." What I didn't realize was that this attitude was holding me back, because I wasn't aware of how much time I was actually spending doing those tasks.

Delegation is all about passing off tasks to others so that you can have more time to do the things that no one else but you can do.

I started to realize that if I had somebody that I could share information with, who could take care of certain daily tasks, I would have extra time to develop other ideas or meet with more people.

It was really hard to make the switch into delegation mode. But once I started, I was hooked. I started wondering, "What else can I delegate? What else is there? Let me just delegate everything. Can I just delegate everything?"

I'm going to share with you a great exercise that I did to answer this very question.

I took a piece of paper, and I wrote down every task I did, all day long, in both my business life and my personal life, from the mundane to the specialized.

Then, I looked at that list and asked myself, "What are the things that I can hire somebody else to do?"

Well, somebody else can't brush my teeth for me, so I have to do that. But somebody else might be able to return phone calls or check email, or set appointments for me, right?

Take a look at all the tasks that you don't want to do, don't have time to do, or shouldn't be doing – and imagine what else you could be doing with that time if you got it back.

When I first made this list, I realized that I was taking a whole day to clean my house, once a week. What else could I do with that 24 hours? To grow my business, grow my family, or make other investments with my time? If I hired somebody to clean my house for 100 bucks a week, I could make that $400 a month in less than a day. When I realized this, delegating the task of cleaning was a no-brainer!

As a leader, you have to ask yourself: How valuable am I? What does my highest contribution to this business/family look like? And why am I doing these low-producing job responsibilities?

When you make that first hire and start to delegate this list, you'll realize how cool it is, and how liberating. It helps you narrow your field of focus to only those tasks that you absolutely love, are passionate about, and are driven to do.

By doing this exercise and moving past the mindset of having to do it all yourself, you now have all this free time to grow your business or invent new companies and products. Remember – you're the entrepreneur, you're the visionary, and you need to find the people that can help you get to the next level in your business and vision.

OUTSOURCE YOUR HIRING AND FIRING

Have you ever hired people, spent all this time and money training them, and they ended up stealing your ideas, becoming your competition, or you end up having to fire them? How do we get over that? How do we think differently?

For me, I've made a lot of mistakes when it comes to hiring people.

I remember after the Great Recession when hiring one of our first buyer's agents, we were drinking margaritas at a Mexican restaurant. Our "hiring process" was something called the mirror test – as in, if we put a mirror under their nose and fog was on it, they were hired. We just needed a warm body. We didn't go through any processes of evaluation that would have actually made a huge impact on our decision. The girl we hired to represent our brand image was driving a car that was half dented in on one side, and we had no idea. How could we send her out to appointments? This is just one example of our negligence when it came to hiring. I was notorious for my bleeding heart and learned very quickly that you don't hire based on feeling sorry for someone, hiring a friend because they need income, or based on one interview without checking references.

It took all these mistakes and horrible processes for us to realize how to do it right. And we're not perfect, but at least we know what to do if we hire somebody that ends up not being who we thought they were. We just know we have to get rid of them pretty quickly.

Ultimately, what works best is to allow other people to hire for you. Have multiple recruiting website platforms that are seeking to find a match equal to your values and tribe, and adding an in-house recruiter who helps expand your team. They're responsible for making first communication with potential team members. They do all the important research on a prospect's social media, their references, their past performance, if they've job hopped, etc. This is an example of a task that I don't have time to do, nor do I want to do. They bring a level of diligence to an area where I might have just said, "Oh, you're cute. Your outfit's cute. You're breathing. Come on. Sure. Yeah, you'll be great at this."

If you have people that recruit for you, you have no vested personal interest – it's business. I want to work around people that have the same hustle as I do, who don't bring gossip and drama around. The recruiters and your team tribe are able to identify those people who are a match to the company ecosystem while keeping a healthy distance between their personal lives and mine.

Of course, you have to have empathy and care about people, because your business isn't going to grow without your passion for people and community. But when it comes to hiring people, I recommend that you hire slow, and have somebody else do it. Work with a recruiter who's like the FBI – who's going to dig deep in the background of each potential employee, to make sure your company and image are represented at the highest level.

Another key part of hiring is having the right contracts in place, from the get-go. This is absolutely essential in any business. What contracts do is protect you from what I call the "copypreneur" – someone who comes in to work for you, learns your trade secrets, and then goes off and does their own thing with everything you've taught them.

I've definitely been through this. And the dilemma I faced was if I've got so much passion to help people, why would I hold anything back? How can I grow other people and help them become leaders if I don't share with them everything I know?

Creating thorough contracts and non-disclosure agreements, which state that yes, we're going to share all of our knowledge, and educate you to be the best person that you can be. We're going to grow you and your mindset. You can go think differently all you want when you leave, you just can't take our product. You can't take our literature. You can't take our systems, taglines, and so on. You can't take our company brand image and use it. Having the proper documentation is about putting the right boundaries in place so that you can be an open book with your team.

These days, I never worry about copypreneurs. I know that if somebody outside of the company sees something that we've done, and they try to incorporate it themselves – they're not me. They're not us. They're not our company. They may adopt a piece of our service, but when they have to show up to perform at the full level of the service, they don't know how that operates. They would never be able to sell on that experience or teach on that experience, because they don't really know it. They just copied it off a social media post or off of a flyer or something like that.

I am my brand, and no one else can be me. When I realized this, I was able to let go of the fear that someone was going to steal my information. I made the choice not to hoard my knowledge, but to share it, because it's what I'm here to do. I'm here to educate the community and create with other leaders.

When you think of a popular sporting team, you think of one or two-star players, right? Those star players are actually the brand. If a team is not doing well and doesn't have star players who lead the team to success, are people going to show up and pay money to watch them? Or wear their numbers on the back of their shirt? No, they're not. The star players that they bring on to the team become the brand. The sports team itself is just like a company – at most, it has a logo and a name – but the heart and soul of the brand are its people.

CHAPTER 2:: GET OUT OF YOUR OWN HEAD

How are you showing up? How is your brand showing up? It's us, the brand that is showing up to lead the community. You have to realize the difference.

When somebody sues somebody, they technically go after the company, but they're going after the person that is attached to the company. That's the image and the brand, and it's where all the value truly lies. That being said, being a leader is about being responsible for your brand image. I am very stern and strong about any association we have with an outside source, vendor, or event. If it's going to hurt my image, I can't move forward. Regardless if it's personal or business, my image and my name are all I have, and I don't want anybody to ever ruin that for me. We're going to be going deeper into branding and image throughout this book.

If you've hired somebody before and it blew up in your face, I understand. It's happened to me. I've mis-hired. I've mis-fired. I have made the wrong decisions. I invested in people that turned out not to go for the long term. But as a business leader, you have to keep going and you have to keep investing in people because ultimately, you're only going to go as far as you can with a team.

TRAIN YOUR TEAM LIKE YOU MEAN IT

The next phase of team-building is onboarding and training. We have systems, training, mentoring, accountability, daily huddle calls, and weekly collaboration meetings. (Notice I call them "collaboration" meetings. Who enjoys going to a sales meeting that, week after week, becomes redundant? Your work tribe wants to have a voice and share ideas, so collaborate. Be open to listening and taking action.)

Every company has a different leader and a different visionary, so their approach to business is going to be different. And so, the first thing that you want to establish with your new employees is, don't bring your past relationships into our current relationship. We're going to teach you how we do it, how our systems work and get you familiar with our mindset so that you can create a different lifestyle for yourself while you're here. Our intention is that you're going to grow in your personal life and your business life through being associated with us.

In the real estate business, most aren't training. They're just giving advice here and there. They're not hands-on, and they're not coaching and educating. And if they are, their material is usually so dated. When we bring on new team members, we encourage them to keep an open mind and pretend they know nothing.

At the end of our bootcamp, everybody says, wow, I've been doing this business for X amount of time, and I've learned more in a week than I've learned in years. And it doesn't stop there! After the initial bootcamp process, our agents can go out to appointments and meet people and start engaging as our brand. After that, we're doing daily training. We're doing daily huddle calls, daily accountability calls, role-playing, all that hands-on and learning through repetitiveness. Because we're always learning and growing.

CHAPTER 2 :: GET OUT OF YOUR OWN HEAD

If you're not learning and growing, you're going to be stuck, and you're not going to like what you're doing. You're going to be uneducated, and you're not going to show up. You're going to burn out because you're running in circles. We only grow when we show up.

A big reason that our training works is because I myself am always showing up to my own training. I like being up to speed, keeping my processes and practices fresh, and going through them myself so I understand my business from the inside out.

A key principle of mine is that I wouldn't ask anybody to do something I've never done. I'm going to go learn it, and I'm going to try it first, and then I'm going to share it. We're going to teach it, we're going to coach it, we're going to implement it. You can never assume that somebody knows what they're doing if you haven't taken the time to train them, or if you don't allow them to ask questions.

You need to create leaders, teach them the processes, and allow them to hold certain pillars of your company – like recruiting, admin, and sales. As we've spoken about, you can't take it all on yourself. Having people moving all the different parts of your process forward and keep asking yourself how you can delegate. Each team member carries a torch of responsibility in the company that supports the rest of us to do our jobs to the fullest.

LEAD WELL AND THEN LET IT GO

The biggest thing about hiring people and building your tribe is the idea of what a team really is. There's no "I" in team, and there's no "me" in team, and that's huge. We watch for that. When someone brings the attitude of "Me and my," versus "Us and ours," that sticks out like a sore thumb to me.

For instance, a past agent with no prior real estate experience made over $100k in the first year on the team. The individual was fast-tracked by the experiences, knowledge, systems, and coaching provided by my previous 21 years in the business.

However, ego turned this agent from grateful to destructive. She left the company with an entitled attitude that she had just landed at the arrival gate.

At first, it was hard, because I took it so personally. I literally lay in bed crying, thinking, what have I done? What did I do wrong? What's wrong with me? Oh my gosh, I did everything for this person, they were struggling, they were about to go through a divorce, they were financially upside down, I paid for them to learn this business. I gave them everything, and man, they shit on me a year later.

But then I realized that it wasn't about me. They made that choice. I know what I did to help them, and I can be happy for what I did during the time that I had to lead them. Now it's somebody else's turn to lead them, whether they're leading themselves or somebody else is leading them, but it's not about me anymore.

We all make business decisions. If someone you work with makes the decision to go off on their own with everything you've given them, you can only wish them luck.

I had to learn that lesson quite a few times. Sometimes people get greedy or feel entitled, or are operating based on deeper things going on in their personal life. Usually about six to 12 months into working with someone, you realize these spots on people. You don't know what's going to happen until you see what's coming forward.

By recognizing that their choices are about them, you can relax into being who you are. You can continue to choose to be a giver. You're choosing to be a leader. And how you show up has nothing to do with how anyone else shows up.

I'm passionate about coaching other people. I'm passionate about giving support and sharing my knowledge. And I've learned to look at these experiences differently, in order to grow stronger and wiser from them.

Generally, women are also wired to have more of a motherly, caring instinct that can often get muddled when it comes to making business decisions. For me, the heartache I felt was like, oh my gosh, we helped them create this lifestyle that they didn't have before. And then, in the end, I don't want them to fail.

It's important to get clear that when someone has their own agenda going, you can't save them or stop them from following that path. Luckily, I've learned how to tell if someone on my team is thinking about making an exit. I know the look. I know the attitude. I know when people start drifting away, where their production stops, and I can sniff it out quickly. If you already know an exit is coming, you can be prepared for it – or save them the trouble by making the exit for them. When you get good at that process, you're unstoppable.

When I decide to exit a person from the company, we have certain systems in place that make the process smoother and easier. Namely, you want to have people who can do the firing for you. I've learned that, just like hiring, firing isn't my strong suit. I used to keep someone longer than I should because I felt sorry for them. Now I've learned that if I'm keeping someone in a position where they're not performing well, I'm holding them back.

What good am I doing for them, if I am waking up every morning thinking about how bad of a job they're doing? Or going to bed at night, with the last thing in my head, being how bad of a job they're doing? How can I be the right leader, if I'm not just nipping it in the bud?

Now, our executive team that does the onboarding also does the offboarding. They'll have a conversation with the employee, contractor, or vendor and say, "Hey, you know what? We're holding you back. We don't have you in the best position, that we think you're more passionate about X and Y."

When it comes to deciding whether or not to keep someone in the company, I've learned to ask myself, what do they want?

- What do you see as the perfect job?
- What do you see as a perfect day of going to work? Identify if they understand the day and life of the company – the true day-to-day operation before they show up for day one.

These are all great questions to ask someone, to make sure that they're actually where they are best suited. There's no use being disappointed in someone's performance if you're the one who's turning a blind eye to what's really in their best interests.

In the last 21 years, I've paid probably 17 personal and/or business checks towards family, friends, or past clients to help them get their real estate license so that they could come into my company and create a different lifestyle. I had an "A-ha!" moment when my daughter said, "Mom, I don't want to be in real estate. You paid four times for me to go to real estate school and I've backed out all four times. This is your dream, not mine."

What I learned from this was that I wanted it more than they did. I may have been disappointed in how things turned out, but they weren't responsible for my feelings – I was trying to push them into a job, and create this entire lifestyle for them that they weren't interested in. They liked how it would look if they pictured themselves driving that car or living in that house, but they didn't show up to that dream the way I had it laid out for them.

You have to be true to yourself, but you have to be true to other people. Ask the right questions to make sure they're going to show up where you need them to show up. And know that it's okay to not hire somebody. You don't hire everybody that comes in your door.

Business is a great teacher in this way. It shows you what you can't see in yourself. And it also helps other people see what they need to see in themselves.

When it comes to the desire to want to help and take care of others, I've learned to spread it around in everything I do.

What I've realized with past relationships across the board is that we're all wired differently, we have different ways of expressing ourselves, different chemical compositions, and different perspectives. I'm a very emotional person, and I've learned that all emotions come from these two main emotions, which are hate and love.

If I'm angry, pissed off, I'm in hate. I'm pacing back and forth, my body cringes, and I can feel my face wrinkle, just saying the word "hate."

But if I say, "I love you," and I smile, I feel my whole body relax. I'm not pacing anymore. I'm looking at the beautiful blue clouds. The trees are blooming, the rose bushes are blooming, they smell great. Now I'm happy and cheerful again because that's love.

It feels like if I smile at you, you're going to smile back at me. If I nod my head, you're going to nod. If I'm all positive, and I'm saying yes, you're going to say yes. I'm smiling, you're going to smile back at me. I don't care how bad your day is. If I looked at you and I smile big, and I show my pearly whites, you're going to smile back. You're not going to understand why you smiled back, but you're going to mirror it.

You have to choose how you're going to show up in life, regardless of where your past has brought you. You have to recognize that the people around you are reflections of what you're bringing. Do you want to be around haters or do you want to be around lovers? It starts with you making that choice for yourself of how you want to show up, regardless of everyone else. Then life will mirror that back to you. You might go through a roller coaster, but it's always your choice to come back to love.

I lived with pain and hate for so long, that sometimes it tries to come back. When it does poke its head in, my catchphrase is simple: "Not today."

What I do is I get in my car, I turn on my favorite '80s music, I roll my windows down and I sing as loud as I can. I have one other song that I play, thanks to Carrie Underwood, and it's "Champion." I'm a champion, and that is my walk-on song. That is my theme song. I'm a champion, I'm unstoppable, and I'm just going to keep going. And so, I can turn my moment around, from that "Not today," really quick.

It all comes from understanding myself on a deeper level, knowing that I am influenced by my experiences, but never controlled by them. I am in the driver's seat of my life and my business – and so are you.

As a business leader, you have to let others in. When you do that, be prepared to learn and to grow, because other people are also going through their stuff, and each relationship will reflect back to you new lessons and opportunities to come to more understanding and empathy. No matter how bad or disastrous it may have been, you become a better leader with every relationship.

Whenever you don't understand something, go understand it. Set yourself in somebody else's shoes. If you can't step in those shoes yourself and try to understand it, there are books, movies, Netflix, neighbors, and friends. Somebody along the way has gone through that path and can help you understand it. Google. Understand it. Educate. Learn.

The bigger you get – and I had to learn this the hard way – the more court cases you might have to show up at. When people realize that you're successful, they're going to try to find ways to take your money. One wise man told me that, "Do you think Home Depot doesn't have lawsuits every day? Home Depot has lawsuits every day. Multiple lawsuits per day." Big companies have lawsuits every day. There have been situations like that for my company which, I had to learn, weren't personal. Somebody found a way that they thought they could make some extra money, and thought, hey, let me see if this will work. If it does, I'll make a couple of bucks off of it.

Some people have taken our business name to try to grow their business. You have to understand that, legal battles can happen when people try to copy you or try to manifest what they see you doing. Always be prepared for that. Make your name big enough and your team strong enough, so that when people want to try to find a way to take you down, you just keep building it up bigger and bigger.

You might be thinking, "Well, if I'm going to be successful like that, I can't be caring, and I can't be fun. I'm not meant for this, I don't have tough skin."

Yes, you do.

The painful experiences that come with running a business are all here for you to learn from. On my journey, I put more energy into researching and understanding my situations, so that I didn't need to keep manifesting the same painful experiences over and over again. I just got out. I said, "I surrender. I don't need any more harsh experiences. I'm

CHAPTER 2:: GET OUT OF YOUR OWN HEAD

just going to go forward with what I know now." Granted, painful lessons are part of the process, but once we learn from our own circumstances – or from observing the experiences of others – we can move on and do things better, with more ease, alignment, and grace.

A leader isn't just born, a leader is formed through life, and through situations and circumstances.

And a leader must be willing to create other leaders, to share their knowledge and wisdom with others. When you get out of your head and start building a team the right way, you can give all the love and passion that you have in your heart. You can learn how to trust people by setting up systems that support you and protect your creative property. And you can help all those around you rise to the next level alongside you.

CHAPTER 3:

BEYOND YOUR MILLION DOLLAR BRAND

In this chapter, I'm going to help you understand what a brand really is so that you can leverage the true power of your brand and business.

To put it simply: Your brand isn't just your logo. Your brand is the experience that people have with the people behind your logo. It includes your image, how you identify with the community, how you network and build rapport with others, and how you show up for the people that you serve.

We've just gone through all my tried-and-tested approaches around hiring, firing, and delegating. You've learned that in order to grow past the million dollar hustle, you have to get out of your head and let people help you. Those same people on your team are a critical part of your brand. They represent you, your product, your service, and the rest of your team. No matter if you're running a tight crew of 3-10 people or a global organization of hundreds. Proper branding is all about getting your entire team on the same page from the start– aligning your values, understanding your messaging, and ensuring that everyone is showing up as a true representation of your brand.

It's only from this place of truly understanding your brand that you can attract those soulmate clients who are meant to work with you, and the more authentic your brand is, the more business you can bring in. By aligning with your brand values, you are going to naturally attract others who also have those same values, and they will feel it when they connect with your brand.

When most companies start out building a brand, they get excited about the "fun stuff" – picking a logo, a name, a font, and colors for their website. Maybe they work with a digital marketing agency, who comes up with a "brand board" of aesthetic images to represent the brand identity. Photoshoots are scheduled, business cards are printed, and boom! A brand is born. It seems easy.

Have you experienced this?

The look of your brand is just a small fraction of what your brand actually is. I've seen a lot of people get confused with this principle. A brand is not its logo, font, and colors. It is the owner, the staff, their salespeople – everybody under the umbrella of that logo and those fonts. You get bad reviews, that's your brand. It's not your logo. It's you. You are your brand.

I've been there, myself. Before I understood what the word "brand" really meant, I thought it was my company name and logo. I thought, "Oh, I've got to come up with a name for my brand. What am I going to name it?" Across the board in every company, branding comes down to, "I've got to think of a name. That's fun. I'm going to think of the logo. That's fun. And the font," that kind of stuff.

Have you ever gone through a "rebrand"? Most people, when they rebrand, start with their logo and their colors. Most don't look under the hood to examine what exactly isn't selling, resonating, or attracting the right client. Maybe they've even had a roll of negative reviews that are making them question their branding.

They forget that they wouldn't have had to rebrand, had they taken the time to understand what their brand was in the first place. It's so much bigger than what most people think it is. Had they provided the best service, the best cost, the best value, the best experience, they probably never would have had to rebrand.

At the beginning of my brand, I was straight up just following the trends. Twenty years ago, the trend in fonts and logos was scrolls, flourishes, script. So I did that; I had all this scrolly stuff in my brand identity for maybe 10 years. Then, as trends changed, I thought, "Oh, I have to rebrand again, because now we're using bold font." I thought I had to keep up with the trends like that – forever! But eventually, after many years of business experience, I realize, "Wait a minute. I could make my logo red and green and put three dots on it. And nobody would care!" Clients weren't flocking to my office to compliment me on my font choice. They were coming to me for my exemplary service, and for the pleasure of working with me and my team.

A logo can definitely make a good impression, and in many cases, it absolutely can add to brand value. That's where Louis Vuitton did a really good job. Their brand is their logo. But at the end of the day, it's still the experience of connecting with the Louis Vuitton brand that matters. I mean, I probably got 50 Louis Vuittons, between shoes and belts, and purses, and backpacks, and luggage. When I first started buying Louis Vuitton, what was I buying? The logo. I wanted to be cool and impress people with the logo.

Now, I don't even care if the logo falls off. Half of my Louis Vuitton items don't even have a visible logo on them. The point for me is that I feel good when I wear it, I feel good when I buy it, and that's all because I enjoy the quality of the experience of shopping with them. They offer this personalized experience that speaks to who I am as a consumer, and I come back time and time again for more of that experience. Even during COVID, the LV sales rep called me and said, "Hey, I'm thinking about you. I got this new design coming in. I know you'll want it, so I'll let you know when it comes in. I just wanted to touch base, see how you're doing, how your family's doing." They know me by name in like five or six different cities!

Luxury brands across the board tend to do this well. I have the Gucci in Atlanta calling me, because they know I love their jewelry, and when I pick up the phone they're like, "Girl, we got this new ring, I'll send you a picture of it." I love these brands because I love that experience of feeling known, cared for, and connected with.

Dunkin' Donuts and Starbucks both serve coffee. At the end of the day, coffee is coffee – but I choose Starbucks because I care about how I feel when I'm in the store. Starbucks does a great job of creating an experience where the coffee tastes great, the ambience is nice, I'm called by name, and they put care into making sure my drink comes out the way I want it. I love Dunkin' Donuts coffee, but they mess my order up every time I go.

We have lots of creative choices that we can make in every type of business. Have fun with those choices, but don't get hung up on what the name of the company is, or the colors and the font and the logo. I can't stress this enough: it's about the experience.

Your company should be completely based upon the client experience, and the creator of the client experience is YOU.

In my case, people don't really know the brokerage firm name, they know my name, and that's the brand. They know me, my face, my voice, and the experience associated.

As a business owner, you are the creator of your client experience. You are what clients will remember about your brand. This means that when you make a mistake, they remember you as well. Your image, the way you treat people, the value that you give, all of that is your brand. You are your brand across the board. You're branded every day, and not just in business.

We are in a society where people judge, and when you're out and about, people will judge your brand image. It's not always a pleasant experience to be judged, but you can use this knowledge to your advantage.

You represent millions of dollars of value. Since you are your brand, you have to show up in alignment with that value, and with what you truly stand for. What is your core mission? What is your promise? What is your culture?

A simple example of this is, I don't go to the grocery store with my hair not brushed. If I didn't fix my hair, I'll put a hat on it – or I'm not going to the grocery store. It's because if I run into somebody in one of these places, I am the image of my brand, of me. And somebody will be like, "Oh, did you see her? She didn't have any makeup on today, her hair was a mess." I'll be judged because I didn't look the particular way that I like to show up as myself and my brand. If the idea of this feels stressful to you, and you just don't care about how you present yourself in public, I highly encourage you to ask yourself how much you care about the service or the promise that you're offering in your business. You are your brand, and you've got to understand that, and you have to show up as your brand.

If people are constantly judging each other on a personal level, they're definitely doing it on a business level. And that's where reviews come in. Search yourself on Yelp and Google and Facebook, and look at those reviews. If you have more negative reviews than you do positive reviews, that's your brand. Have you noticed that in each strong review, the customer talks about the person that was involved with their experience? The review's basically targeting one person: the cashier, the person that changed my tire.

CHAPTER 3:: BEYOND YOUR MILLION DOLLAR BRAND

I had a negative experience with Cadillac. But my problem wasn't really with Cadillac. My problem was with the people working at the dealership. They ruined that brand, in my opinion, on a $130,000 car I bought, and made my experience rough for nine months. They wouldn't fix it until I said I was going to call the media and have a conversation. Now, I would still go buy another Cadillac but I wouldn't buy it from that dealership, or from anybody that worked there, because of the experience I went through. You buy a nice car, you expect to have a nice experience, right? They were the brand, not Cadillac. I'm good with Cadillac. I'm just not good with the people at that dealership.

Don't make the mistake of hiding behind your logo. Many people think that that's the only thing that people are ever going to look at, see, or judge. They also mistake the logo or the name for carrying the value of the company.

For instance, people know me from the radio. They've seen me on TV. These appearances can be brief, but they provide valuable credibility. I have worked hard to build a positive brand. This helps many viewers and listeners who don't yet know me, to choose to rely on me.

If another person were to use my name or business name, people would be confused. Suppose that company did not provide the same value that we advertise on radio and TV. What if they didn't get someone the equity that we promise, and then that client went and blasted us because they thought that we were the same company? Or, what if a client thought they were doing business with us, and we lost the sale?

Guess who would be blamed for any bad experience? It would be me!

At the end of the day, they may never be able to duplicate our customer experience, which is what it comes down to. It's kind of like Burger King and McDonald's, right? Which one came first and which one copied? But the hamburgers taste different, right? And they use different things to make their brand bigger.

If you drive by Burger King you're going to smell grill charcoal. You're going to smell the flaming charcoal when you go by at Burger King, because they put it out of their vents out of their restaurants. So that when you're across the street from McDonald's and Burger King, you drive by, you smell Burger King charbroiling over there. Because they have a scent that comes out of the rooftop to get you to come over there. So if it smells good and I'm thinking, "Ooh, I want a hamburger," I smell hamburger, I'm going to start tasting it, I'm going to see it. My mouth is going to water. And I'm pulling into Burger King.

But if I drop by and the smell isn't going, because it only runs a few times a day, I'm probably just going to go to McDonald's because it's more convenient on my route.

The point is, I don't go to either place because of their fonts or their logo. Their signs are different, but their sign didn't get me there, right? Their colors didn't get me there. The taste of their product and their experience brought me in. Burger King already had me smelling and eating a hamburger before I went through their drive-through.

They know that their brand is the extension of everything that touches the customer. And I mean, everything. I always say if there's an A, there's a Z, and if there's a beginning, there's an end. I believe that, yes, figuring out your name, identity, and what colors you're going to use, and all that kind of stuff is A.

There's an end to everything that you do from point A, and those Z-points are the places of connection where a human forms a relationship with your brand. To understand this, stop fussing with your colors and fonts, and ask your clients for real feedback on their experience with you. Use that feedback to improve your brand service or promise. Aim for those 4.9, 5-star reviews, and address any negative reviews with care and timeliness.

When I had the other mindset, I changed my logo more times than I can remember because it was never right. But now my brand is so solid, and it's bold, and it's who we are in the community. My main focus is on training our agents and staff in every company to uphold that image. At our clothing store, I've told my team, "You're the image, you are the brand. You are representing Southern Lace Boutique. When people come in here, if you're on your cellphone and you don't talk to them, they're going to remember that experience. If they don't feel welcome, you're representing Southern Lace Boutique. Put your phone down. You can take a break whenever you need to, but you are here to be present, welcoming, and friendly."

When people have a negative experience somewhere, they're going to tell everybody they know. We habitually tell people what we don't like in life more than what we love. And so, their friends may not come and visit us either.

Think about the last time you had a bad experience you had at any place you went to. It's about a person, right? It's not about, you walked in and the logo fell on your head when you walked in Nordstrom. No. It was the experience that you had there. And if you got the size shoes that you wanted, and you looked good wearing them, you left that store feeling good. You had a good experience and you're going to go back. But if you went there and you sat waiting for your shoes and they were helping everybody else, or they were sitting behind the counter on their phone, or they were just totally ignoring you, you're leaving there without your shoes. Now you might go to Neiman Marcus instead.

Another tip I give to my salespeople is not to "be a car salesman" and overkill with the attention they give to each customer. Any car salesmen that read this book, I'm sorry, but y'all often overkill. When I car shop now, I stay in my car. I keep my windows up, and I don't even look in their face. I'm the kind of shopper who's done my research and knows what I want to buy.

So the brand experience I want customers at my clothing store to have is a relaxed, independent shopping trip, where they're not being hustled and upsold.

There's a store that I used to go to at the mall. I'd go in there for one thing and I'd walk out with about 50. Because they always would upsell me, and their goal for that department store was that each salesperson had to sell at least three items. So if somebody was buying one, you better be ringing up three. I'm a woman in sales, but they still got me with the experience of being shown cute outfits that would match whatever I was looking for. They'd be like, "Look at these pants that just came in. Oh my gosh, this is going to look so good on you. You get this one too." And I walk out of there it's like Target. I only go in there, for one thing, I can't leave Target without spending less than 100 bucks. I'm like, "How did that happen?" It's because the experience of shopping at Target is fun. It's clean and well organized, so I'm going to spend a little bit longer there and they have some cute stuff. If I go to Walmart, on the other hand, I buy one thing and get out. They have a lot of similar products, but it's the experience I'm going for. If Walmart created a nicer environment, and I didn't feel dirty when I walked in, I might spend more time and money there.

I don't care what the name of the store is. I care about how I'm treated and how I feel when I'm in there. That's your brand.

Branding is really powerful because it defines what kind of experience you offer, and it absolutely impacts the type of clients you attract.

The people you meet who feel like perfect clients are attracted to you because of what you're putting out there. You likely have similarities in the way you think, how you approach things, or what you like. To put it simply, you are who you sell to.

A big part of your brand experience is storytelling. Storytelling helps you connect with your community and makes it even easier for the right clients to find you. Whether you make videos, do interviews, write books, or get on stage, there are many ways that you and your team can share your relevant personal experiences to build rapport with the people around you.

Human beings are sensitive, empathetic creatures, and we like to be understood. I've learned that if you can put your feet in a lot of different people's shoes, and build rapport through lessons that you've learned along the way, you can attract a lot of different people. There might be people who read this book and think, "Oh, I connect with her. I'm going to find her, and I'm going to do business with her because she'll understand me." But if I don't tell my stories, I might miss valuable opportunities to connect with others. The ultimate reward of storytelling is that it invites your clients to open up and share their experiences with you, too, which makes it easier – and more meaningful – for you to serve them.

In my real estate business, I'm passionate about the goals of the buyers and the sellers, and the way they feel when they show up at closing and they've gotten to their goal in their journey. For many people, buying a house is the American dream. I've been at a closing with a client who was 60 years old. And that was the first house they ever bought. I didn't know this fact during the process until we got to closing. I still get chills thinking about how I felt sitting next to them. They started crying and they said, "You know what? I've never bought a house before." I was like, "Are you kidding me? You didn't share this with me before, are you serious?" She goes, "Yeah, I was always too scared, or didn't have the

CHAPTER 3:: BEYOND YOUR MILLION DOLLAR BRAND

money, or didn't have the credit." And it took this person until they were 60 to feel like they could go for that goal. But they did it, they accomplished it. And what an amazing story we got to share. That's why I do what I do because there's an end game for everybody that calls us.

You can only succeed at building a multi-million dollar brand if you're passionate about your business, and have the client's endgame at heart. As business owners, it's our duty to show up in our community and offer the highest value that we can. For me, this means I don't see sales as though I'm taking something from somebody. I see every transaction I make as a service to my community.

As a real estate expert, if I didn't show up for my business, especially during recessions and pandemics, I'd be hurting my community and the larger ecosystem around us. I know that each transaction isn't really about pocketing cash. It's partly about the buyer and the seller, and being a part of their journey. But it's also about all the other people involved in the process of that journey. I learned this during the second recession that I've been in through this business, from 2008 to 2011. Beyond the buyer and the seller, you have the real estate agent, you have painters, you have attorneys, you have lenders, and you have appraisers, their staff, title companies, you name it. All of these different people benefit from one house sale, and one house sale feeds a lot of people. And so I would be failing my community and this industry if I didn't show up when they needed me the most.

Yes. I mean, and then I look at it as, if I didn't get to that family, that buyer or seller, they might've had a bad experience in the industry, and somebody might have not have treated them the right way because they had commission breath.

They didn't educate and they didn't do the right thing, because they were just worried about running to the bank.

And that happens across the board in sales.

One of my Facebook friends has a very successful roofing company. He's doing good in the community. When he does a roof, he'll go to a local school, and if there are parents that haven't paid for school lunch meals for their kids, and they have outstanding balances, he'll go pay those balances off.

I was scrolling Facebook one morning when I saw that my roofer friend had posted a screenshot of a competitor in the community. The competitor was making fun of his company, because of some ridiculous reason – that all their company trucks are lifted, with big tires.

Along with the screenshot, my friend wrote, "If anybody knows this guy, you might want to go check out some of his other posts on his profile, because y'all are the ones who may do business with him that might get hurt from this. You don't have to do business with me, but I think you should be warned."

I checked out the profile in question and found that he had been bashing my Facebook friend's roofing company for perhaps six months on different things. He even said, "There's another local roofing company in the area who gives money to the schools to pay for lunches. So you know what, I'll do the same. I'll give it to a charity of your choice, but use my service instead."

CHAPTER 3 :: BEYOND YOUR MILLION DOLLAR BRAND

And I was like, "Oh dear God, who does this guy work for? Is this his own company?"

It wasn't. He was representing a company that he worked for, which was the brand. The brand didn't write that message, but this guy was part of the brand, he was the image of that company. His action was causing that brand to lose business. How could anyone trust him to put a $20,000 roof on their house?

You have to remember everybody you hire is your brand too – online and offline. Be on top of your company policies regarding your team's social media presence, and stay aware of how people are perceiving them and their character. Train your team to understand that just one sour post can ruin your entire brand. They all need to step up and look at how their personal brand is impacting the company brand as a whole. And if they're not willing to take ownership and responsibility of what they post, what they say, and even the energy and the conversations that they're bringing in, then they're not representing your brand.

Now that you understand the fundamentals of having a multi-million dollar brand, I want to share another strategy I use for scaling my business and attracting awesome clients who will leave great reviews on my brand.

It's simple: when you work with an ideal client, ask them for referrals to two more people who are just like them. Clients who are pleasant, communicate well, and are easy to work with are often surrounded by other folks with a similar disposition. When I coach someone whom I absolutely love working with, I tell them: "I loved working with you.

I want to work with people just like you. Do you know two people that are just like you, that you could refer to me?"

Not everybody is pleasant to work with, and it's important to know how to respond to them when they show up in your field. Sometimes you meet people who have gone through really hard times, who don't know the love side of life. To them, nagging is normal, everything is disappointing, and all the bad shit happens to them. For me, I've been there, and I no longer tolerate that vibration of upset and rudeness in myself, in my family, or in my business.

If a client screams at me over the phone, you better believe I'm not going to ask them for a referral, because I already know that we attract our tribe and that anyone they send my way is probably going to be a nightmare, too.

Instead, I'm going to attract more people that are going to be positive and pleasant to work with. It's a marker of true success when you can actually walk out of an appointment and say, "I don't need to work with that person, because I don't need that money that bad."

I bring my value to the table every time, and I never worry if clients are sussing out the competition or trying to haggle me down because I'm not competing against anyone.

When a prospective client tells me, "I'm interviewing other agents (or coaches)," I say, "I completely agree with you because I don't work with everybody either. I have to make sure that we're going to work well with one another. And so I'm here interviewing you, just like you're interviewing me."

And guess what? When I make that distinction, now the prospect and I are on a whole new level of understanding.

We're not competing against each other. We're now going to respect each other and decide if it's a good relationship for both of us.

I wake up every day, wanting to work with people that I want to be around. I don't want to look at my phone and cringe because I have to talk to somebody I don't want to talk to. When we're on the million dollar hustle, we gotta sell everything. We gotta kiss butt, we gotta clean up shit. We gotta do lots of stuff that we don't want to do.

Beyond a million, we don't do that anymore. I can fire somebody quick if they're going to disrespect us. If they disrespect anybody in our tribe. We're not going to do it, we don't need to do it, and it's not healthy to do it.

One of my employees was taking verbal abuse from a customer without my knowledge. One day she happened to be telling me a story about how this customer was just screaming at her, first thing in the morning, and that it just ruined her day. I was like, "Girl, what?" And she goes, "Oh yeah, all the time. People yell at me."

I go, "What? I don't know why you didn't tell me this."

I had no idea it was going on. She had just been tolerating it, time and time again. And I said, "No. We don't tolerate this. This is what you're going to say, and I need you to write this down: 'I'm sorry, Mr. or Mrs. so-and-so. I don't understand the way that you're treating me right now and can't communicate with you while you're speaking like this. I'm going to hang up. Can you please call me when we can have a professional conversation?' And hang up. Mr. Click It, just

Mr. Click It. You already gave him a warning that you were hanging up. Click! We're out."

How you and your team communicate says everything about your brand. Have you ever been to Chick-fil-A? Chick-fil-A's employees all say, "My pleasure." I could go poop on their floor, and they would clean it up. And I would say, "I'm sorry," And they would say, "My pleasure." And I'm thinking, " 'I just shit on your floor, and you just said 'My pleasure.' " That's the way that the Chick-fil-A brand communicates.

When I go to Disneyland, I love walking down Main Street. Every day is a beautiful day on Main Street. I could throw up on the sidewalk on Main Street after getting on a roller coaster, and Disney staff would clean it up as happy as a lark. Mary Poppins would come over and hand me a lollipop, I'm sure. That's fun. I want to be on Main Street, USA, every freaking day.

And I want my clients to be on Main Street every day. There's a difference between Main Street, USA, and Shit Street, USA, all day long. And I don't want to ride on Shit Street. My GPS says, "Exit Shit Street – right now."

By now I'm sure you've realized that some people just don't give a damn about their brand experience. But I do, and it comes from understanding that the experience I create for my clients can leave a permanent imprint on their lives.

This goes for all our relationships. At the end of the day, the way you make people feel is what they remember about you. For example, there's one childhood memory that comes up for me almost every day. I was a young girl learning cursive in school, and I was so excited. And I remember that my mother told me that I had the worst handwriting that she had ever seen in her life.

And so every time I sign my name, or I write something, it comes up. Now I think it's funny because more people have told me in life, "Oh my God, you have awesome handwriting." And I'm like, "That's not what my mom thought."

Remember situations where you weren't treated well, and learn not to make anybody else feel the way that you don't want to feel. I remember all the things that my ex-husband put me through, or the bullying I experienced in school and how bad it made me feel. I don't want to be that person. This part of my brand reflects my character and my morals.

I used to say all the time, "I will never be my mother." I love my mother, but I will never behave like my mother because I didn't like the way that she made me feel. She didn't tell me she loved me, she didn't give me hugs. We didn't have a bond. Because of the pain I experienced from that, I know that I should not make anybody feel less worthy of who they are and their identity in their life. It's an old saying, you treat people the way you want to be treated. You can't fake genuine care and compassion, and that's what I stand for.

If I know that somebody is bullshitting me, if I know that somebody doesn't care about their service, and they're just doing it for a sale, I walk. I've been through it and hurt that way. And I would never want to do that to somebody else. Know your value when it comes to how you treat other people. Your clients will be able to smell your bullshit a mile away.

Bullying is another thing to watch out for. Sometimes it can be happening right under your nose, and it's your responsibility to become aware of it and bring it to an end.

Last week, one of our sales agents had a closing. She earned her income, and she got to closing, and the other agent did something, paperwork-wise, that wasn't right, which took away some of our agent's income. On top of that, the seller didn't disclose some fees that would be due for her HOA, to the tune of $750. And then the seller wanted to make my agent pay that $750, for a mistake that they made when they filled out their own paperwork.

My agent was bullied by the other agent and our client, and I wasn't aware of it. This happened on Thursday, and I didn't find out about it until Monday.

I asked her, "Why didn't you call me?" And she replied, "Because they were bullying me, and it was easier for me just to give it, just to pay it."

I said, "You know what? This money comes out of your pocket. It doesn't come out of my pocket. But here's the problem: you worked really hard, you did your job, and you have value. You need to stick up for yourself. And if that seller had said, 'If you don't pay this, I'm not going to close right now,' you should have said, 'Okay then.' Because that seller would have been in breach of contract and we would have handled it a different way. She was bullying you over something that wasn't your fault, and you gave in. And so now you just lost $1,250 for your family. That's your lifestyle and your earnings."

CHAPTER 3 :: BEYOND YOUR MILLION DOLLAR BRAND

I made her call the other agent's broker and tell them what had happened. After that, we had another conversation. I asked her about what she learned.

She said to me, "You could have just said, 'Oh, well, learn your lesson,' and been done with it. Because it didn't come out of your pocket. It came out of my pocket. But you cared enough about me for it to never happen again. And if I didn't know what steps to take or what to say, I'd probably fall into the same trap."

She continued, "It was hard, but I felt so much better after I called that other broker to tell them what their agent had done. Next time, I'm just going to take a step back. And I'm going to say, 'Okay, fine, don't close. You'll be in breach of contract and we'll handle it later.' I'm not going to give in because I knew I wasn't the one that made the mistake."

It was a good lesson and a reminder for both of us.

It's important to empower your team to deal with all these different kinds of misbehavior, so that they understand how to respond to shady situations in integrity, on behalf of your brand.

We've covered a lot in this chapter, and by now you should have a much deeper understanding of what a brand is. Now, I want to invite you to take the time to reflect and do an inventory on your own brand:

Are you overly fixated on the look and feel of your logo and fonts?

Is everyone on your team acting in accordance with your brand values?

Where in your business can you become more clear, more solid, more bold in what you will and will not tolerate?

How deeply do you really care about your customers, and is that reflected in your reviews?

Are you dealing with clients who aren't treating you well? How can you end those cycles of bullying and start attracting your dream clients?

Remember, we're going beyond a million dollar brand here. A fancy name and flashy storefront aren't enough. You want people to rave about the experience of working with you; the quality, depth, and care that you offer. And it all comes from who you are inside. Because at the end of the day, your brand is you.

CHAPTER 4:
YOU ARE YOUR OWN COMPETITION

We grow up with a competitive mindset in almost everything we do, from grades in school to business revenue, sales, and acquisitions. I used to constantly follow my "competitors," until I realized that doing so was a complete waste of my time. Now, I know that I am my own – and only – competition.

In this chapter, I'm going to share with you more about my philosophy of being your own competition, and examples of how you can truly live and work on your own terms, free from the trap of what anyone else is doing or saying. If you're always focused on the haters, you're not doing everything you can to innovate, create, and grow past the million dollar hustle. The most important place you can put your attention and energy is into your own learning, your own passion, and the contribution you want to make to the world through your business and brand.

For me, shifting out of the mindset of competitiveness was a gradual thing. It happened because I was naturally interested in my growth, and how I could learn and improve on what I was doing, rather than trying to copy or exceed what anyone else was doing. I know that not everyone is driven to learn and innovate, but if you're a business owner like me, chances are that impulse to learn is already ingrained inside you.

We've all been trained to compete. Many coaches I've had in the past have advised me, "Research your competition. Who is your competition? Know your competition. Know what they're doing."

What I found out was, my "competition" was still doing what they were doing 10 years ago or 20 years ago. So if I do what my competition does, and they never grow, and I'm just a copypreneur off of them, how am I going to excel? How am I going to grow myself? People who are on this tribe with me, in my family, how are we going to grow? If you're just copying your competition, then you're just going to be copying average.

Like many people, I was playing this game – the average game. I suffered from all the feelings of being not good enough, not successful enough, and getting jealous and demotivated when other people would do better than me.

One day, after several years of leaving the competitive mindset behind, I had somebody ask me, "Who's your

CHAPTER 4:: YOU ARE YOUR OWN COMPETITION

competition?" And it just came out of my mouth: "I'm my own competition."

When I heard myself say those words I was like, "Wow, Tracy. You just shared some wisdom that you didn't even realize you had learned on your own."

It was a total A-ha moment for me. I asked myself, "When did I get to this place? When did that happen?" I went and looked back at our business performance around the time that I had stopped thinking about other people, and it clicked. I had been preaching about my haters, saying, "If these people would stop focusing on my results, they would probably just be as productive as me."

I wasn't aware that I had been doing just that – focusing on my productivity instead of on others. No wonder I got out of that million dollar hustle! I think about how much energy my haters spend on watching me, and not being productive, and I know that if they took that energy and used it to focus on themselves, they would be so much further in life.

There are so many reasons why people are haters. At the end of the day, I could see that behind their jealousy and shit talk, they just weren't showing up. I was the one showing up, and so that's why they were hating. When I became aware of this, I surrendered to not listening to them at all.

People use the saying all the time, "Stay in your lane," as advice for success, and it's true. If you stay in your lane, don't get distracted, don't go off the exit ramp, don't do a U-turn, don't go back to the crap that you left behind, you'll keep going down the endless road of success.

When it comes to real estate, I couldn't tell you who else is in the business, last month, this month, or a year ago, unless we're currently working with them. I'm focused on the bigger picture. I'm focused on the things that matter the most to me, and that is my family, my clients, and my community – not what everybody else is doing. The truth is, I don't care. That's their journey, not mine.

When your only competition is you, you'll start to see the ways in which you settle for being "average." A lot of people who are trapped in the fear of how they look compared to others are keeping themselves stuck at average.

Average people don't like for other people to be more than average. They like to see people in pain. They love to gossip and they love to see failure because they don't ever want anybody to go above them. And when I went through that transition of deciding that I no longer was going to be average, it physically hurt to feel and release all of that discouraging, stuck energy in me that had built up from years of people talking down to me. People can get so stuck because other people kick them down. They don't encourage them to grow, because how would it make them look if somebody else rose above them?

In my eyes, average people want others to stay average because they have no self-development, they have no self-interest or growth, or don't want to help other people in their passion. Their journey is so lost that they have no inspiration. I know I was wired that way before, but I don't understand it now. I got rid of what I fear and trained my mind to believe

CHAPTER 4:: YOU ARE YOUR OWN COMPETITION

and think differently about myself, so I can't go back into those limiting mindsets anymore.

There was a Disney movie called "Inside Out", and it was all about the different fear and emotions that live in your subconscious mind, and whenever you have a conscious thought, your subconscious mind goes back and finds those emotional memories. I relate to this because I feel these little cartoons going around in my own head – these little file folders, all of these different reactions and responses stored in my memories. If I stub my toe, my subconscious mind thinks, "Oh, when Tracy stubs her toe, what does that feel like? PAIN!"

But most of the time, does it really even hurt? NOPE. So it's a cycle. You stub your toe, you autopilot the association to pain.

Time to break the cycle, rewire stubbing your toe and laughing. They say it takes 14 days to change a habit. So stub your toe for the next 14 days repetitively and just bust out a contagious laugh immediately.

By day 14, you are now rewired to laughing when you stub your toe.

I've done a lot of repatterning and reprogramming of my subconscious mind, and so sometimes I can't even find memories of my past pain or trauma. I love it because I don't even want to remember that pain. Once I've learned from it, I choose to continue to only remember certain things about my experiences because that keeps my mind available for new growth and expansion.

When you're done being average, you're done. All you know is that other people are still stuck, and you used to be stuck, but you can't even remember why. When you can't even remember why, that's how you know you've transformed.

Think about the clock-in, clock-out mindset. "They" say that the average we're supposed to work is eight hours a day, and we're supposed to get our average eight hours of sleep, and while we're at it, drink an average of eight glasses of water. Who made that up? I know a lot of people that might only have to work three hours a day and they accomplish a lot. I'll recommend that you drink more water than not. But when did we, as a society, become comfortable with the average time per day that somebody should work? That doesn't make any sense to me. I've come in contact with people in my past that are clock-in clock-out mode when it comes to work, and it seems that mindset spills out into everything else they do. It's great to have a schedule, but it's one thing to know that your schedule does not only operate between eight and five, and if you have the eight and five mentality, you're unlikely to achieve more success than the "average" paycheck.

While there's nothing wrong with working a set schedule, I know that I have more to offer in life. There's more that I can do. There's more that I can share. When I think of retirement, I'm like, what is that? We think that retirement arrives at a certain age and that we should "stop" then. My life is not stopping because somebody told me that this is the year that I need to retire. No. If I've got it in me, I'm pushing.

CHAPTER 4:: YOU ARE YOUR OWN COMPETITION

You've got one life to live and you have to live it to its fullest. I don't know if I have tomorrow. And so I'm going to show up every day, take the opportunities I've been given, and live my journey to the fullest.

To create a multi-million dollar business, you have to let your creative energy flow whenever it wants to. I'm so inspired about my business and solving problems that it's just flowing from me all the time. Sometimes I stay up all night thinking about new things to implement. I'll see something and think, "Oh, I can 100x that idea." And so I can't wait to get it going. Most of the time, if you look at my laptop, I have 10 browsers opened with 50 tabs on each of them. People will look at that and go, "Oh my God, that makes my head hurt." For me, I love it – because that's all the stuff I want to learn. And if my computer dies or it turns off, I'm like, "Oh my God, all those tabs I had opened that I didn't get to, they're gone." And I always have to go and make sure I can restore them.

Life would be so freaking boring if I never knew that I could work more than eight to five. It was only when I left corporate America that I realized working on my own schedule was better for my brain, and way more fun. I think of the universe as a catalog; there are so many opportunities out there for us. And every moment of your day is a perfect time to take advantage of a new opportunity.

Do you ever get great ideas in the shower? When I wash my hair in the shower, that's a kind of "downtime" for me where I often come up with awesome ideas. I often get great ideas in the shower, and I used to think, "If only I had a marker or lipstick or something to jot this down." Can you guess what I did? I got a dry erase marker that I keep in the shower, and I write on the shower wall as ideas come. Then, when I get out, I take a photo of my notes so I don't forget them. I highly encourage you to adopt this tip if you get creative in the shower, too!

I also can't emphasize enough my love for learning online. When you're fast-paced, creative, and passionate about learning, there's nothing you can't do, be, or get stronger at with the help of the internet.

I was interviewed the other day and they asked me, "What is the biggest difference between how it was when you started in real estate, and now?" And I replied, "The internet."

I didn't have the internet in 1999. I had a Polaroid camera, a black and white copier, and a Sharpie marker, and that's what I used to price and advertise property.

The internet has given us so many opportunities to reach so many people on such a different level. People don't realize that! If you were not in certain businesses and you came in after the internet, you never got to see the other side of it.

I am so intrigued by all the new things I can learn online.

If you've ever heard of this website called lynda.com, it's part of LinkedIn, where you can learn just about anything that you can think of without actually attending a school. For example, I learned how to launch a podcast from lynda.com.

The great breadth and depth of content on the internet reminds me always that we don't know what we don't know until we have to learn it. When I got into the business in

CHAPTER 4 :: YOU ARE YOUR OWN COMPETITION

1999, I didn't know what I didn't know, I just learned to deal with whatever came up – just like we did during this pandemic. We didn't know that we could do listing and buyer appointments via Zoom. We didn't know we could do a whole mastermind group or a whole summit on Zoom. I've met more amazing people through Zoom than I did at live conferences! The world is truly limitless. The experience of COVID-19 has shown me that when we stay open and available to every opportunity, we can grow our business and expand ourselves. Resources like lynda.com help me adapt and learn new things, and that keeps me constantly growing and improving on the skills that I have. If you're a business owner, you can go far with brushing up on a few skills in areas that you're not strong in. Take design, for example. It costs nothing to watch a basic tutorial on Canva or Photoshop, and those skills can go a long way when it comes to reviewing promo materials or social media graphics for your brand.

A lot of people don't think about sharpening their skillset, but it's so important. It's like the mechanical room of your house. When people go to buy a house, and we ask, "What are you looking for in a house?" They don't say, "Oh, I want my HVAC to be amazing. I want my water heater to be amazing." But that's the engine of the house, that's what's heating and cooling and giving you water, and without that engine, you're going to be like, "Oh crap, how do I take a shower? This is cold water, not hot water." Or, "Oh my gosh, it's 90 degrees outside and my air is not working." Or, "It's

20 degrees outside and my heat's not working." When those things happen, your house basically shuts down, right?

So my mind is my engine, and so if I don't keep my engine going, I'm going to mechanically fall apart. If I forget to service my car, it's going to die faster than it would if I continue to tune it up and I continue to service it. So I have to continue to tune my mind and service my mind and learn and grow so that my engine just keeps going because that just keeps creating more ideas, and that's what continues you to grow.

I think that God blessed me with the desire to learn and grow, and He put me through a journey in life to wake up to it. I wasn't a victim, or underprivileged, or stupid, or undeserving – just because I was a bottom-of-the-barrel kind of kid with ADHD, graduating high school with Cs and Ds. Others would tell me, "Man, Tracy, you're so dumb. Where are you ever going to be in life?" But had I known then how I learn now, I would have probably had As and Bs instead.

Once I learned how my mind worked, I just kept challenging myself and kept challenging myself and kept challenging myself, and now, I just can't stop. I just want to know more, know more, know more, and it drives me nuts if I can't figure out how something works. I happily do research, and I actively hire people with more expertise to teach me what they know. At the same time, you'll also hear me say, "I don't want to know how to build the clock. I just to know what time it is." When it comes to certain things, I'm less interested in learning. Take paperwork systems and writing reports, for example. But if it's an invention, or something cool, or marketing, or a message, I want to know all about it.

CHAPTER 4:: YOU ARE YOUR OWN COMPETITION

I want to know the entire outline of how it works and how we're going to get it done.

I think that if you're not intrigued by life, if you don't have passion for something, if you don't have a drive, if you just want the eight to five average workflow, you'll miss out on all the opportunities that you can discover. Doing the same thing every day can eventually lead to depressive feelings, boredom, and hopelessness. I know from my own experience that if you have even a tiny seed of a dream of doing something different than your average, it's not just a dream. It can be a reality if you open up your eyes to it and start digesting the steps that you have to take to get there.

Even though taking the steps towards our dreams can be messy and challenging, having genuine passion is like using rocket fuel that never runs out. When you're passionate, growth is never-ending. When your life doesn't have passion in it, when you don't care about what you do, it feels more like you're slowly dying. I've been there before, but I always had it in me. We all do. Now it feels like there aren't enough hours in a day for me to keep learning and creating everything I want to. And a big secret to this, my greatest motivation, is always to create value for my community, and to bring something meaningful to people's lives.

Every Christmas we pay it forward in our community through the Christmas Wish with a local radio station. People nominate individuals who they think could use some extra support and care, and we get to be a part of fulfilling their Christmas Wish. Every year we have found a single mom or dad who is struggling, and we help them. We pay their bills for months upfront, we refurnish their place, we fill it up with food, we give them Christmas gifts, we decorate for Christmas, we bring cars and TVs and video games and computers, whatever we need to do to help them get back on their feet. We've also given scholarships for a college education.

I've been a struggling single mom. It sucked, and I didn't have help. I didn't have anybody to pick me up. But I also had so much pride and ego that I didn't ask anybody either, and a lot of single moms are the same. I've walked in on many situations for The Wish, where they've had no beds, barely had any food, and if they did, it was expired. I understand that struggle, I feel it intimately, and I also know what a huge boost of motivation and relief comes from having someone show up to help you. I love helping these women show up differently with a better attitude, attracting greater opportunities for themselves and their families.

My goal is to do that once a week. So I help 52 single moms a year get back on their feet, and that is my endgame, that is my goal, that is what drives me every day to get up and do what I do because I've been there.

When you're hustling to make that first million, you're so caught up in your own chaos that it's sometimes hard to see the bigger picture or to find a deeper motivation to serve others. But I want to encourage you to start looking beyond that. Start thinking about what you can do with your success, with your life, with your business to benefit the world around you. It will give you momentum and energy that you can use to make big moves.

CHAPTER 4 :: YOU ARE YOUR OWN COMPETITION

Just like you are your own competition, you are also your own role model. Whenever people ask me, "Who inspires you? Who are your role models?" I don't know what to say. To me, I got here the same way everybody else did – by figuring it out on my own. We just have different choices and different paths that lead us to who we are eventually meant to be. I see people idolize people, like my own kids: they see these Tiktokers or Instagrammers and say, "Oh my gosh, that's so and so."

Yes, there are very powerful people in this universe and they've all done amazing things. I can think of Mother Teresa. I can think of all these amazing people who show up and are loving and passionate about everything they do. They do inspire me to continue to live by my passion, to grow, and learn.

But do I wake up like some people do and think, "Oh my gosh, if I could go meet Oprah that would be the coolest thing ever"? No.

I love Oprah, but if you asked me who I'd have lunch with today if I could ask anyone in the world, my answer would be different every day.

Today it might be the governor of our state. I have some questions about some of his decisions, such as when he reopened the state when we weren't ready at the beginning of COVID.

Tomorrow, I might wake up and choose someone else. I might say, "You know what? I feel like singing country music today. So let's go meet Faith Hill." We'd sing country music at lunch that day – but then the day after that, it would be different.

Who I want to connect with depends on what my journey looks like that day and what I'm trying to accomplish.

One person would probably be the number one person on my list if she were still alive: Princess Diana. She was passionate, she was loving, she was caring, she was a giver. I would want to be around her for five minutes, just to see her interact with the world. I wouldn't even have a question for her – it would just be to get that energy from her.

Just like I don't make decisions based on what my "competitors" are doing, I haven't designed my life or my business around role models or people whom I've idolized. I see myself as my own role model.

At the end of the day, the writing is on the wall – and it's a wall that everybody in the whole world can see. If you visit my website or read my Google reviews, they're not lies, they're not fabricated, they're not billboards that I made up. The stories of real people whose lives my team has been able to help are as real as it gets. Each and every one of those clients means something to me. I feel like a counselor being in the real estate business, because I never know what I'm going to walk into. People have different situations, needs, and dreams.

When we meet a client for the first time, we don't know what their goal is or why they called us. Whether it's losing a family member, getting married, going through a divorce, having a child, getting older and downsizing, every sale has

CHAPTER 4:: YOU ARE YOUR OWN COMPETITION

a story. My heart is totally engaged with my work and with these people. They are my bottom line.

Okay! We've come to the end of this chapter, where we've talked about the average hater and how paying attention to those people is not the way to grow your business. I've shared my passion for learning and growing, and hopefully have inspired you to pursue your own.

I'll leave you with an awesome mindset trick that I learned from a friend of mine, Hal Elrod. Hal taught me the magic of the "miracle morning" mindset. The idea is, you wake up every morning like it's Christmas morning.

Sometimes I picture myself as a child on Christmas morning, so excited to get down the stairs to see what Santa left. Or, I picture myself excited for my kids to wake up Christmas morning because I can't wait to shower them with love and gifts.

If we wake up every day with that miracle morning attitude, life is just so much better. There's so much positivity and so much love to be experienced.

It all comes back to mindset and deciding if you're coming from hate or love. If you just stay in your lane, stay on that love journey, focused on the passion that you have for your life and other people, you don't have to worry about what anybody else is doing. The only thing that matters is you. You are in control of your mindset, choices, journey, and what you will tolerate, or shall I say – what you won't tolerate.

CHAPTER 5:

FROM BURNOUT TO BEACH MODE

(OR, SAYING BYE-BYE TO MILLION DOLLAR BURNOUT)

If you're working 24/7 day after day in any business, you're going to hit burnout mode. Being on the hustle is addictive – trust me, I know – and while it feels like we're accomplishing so much, constantly grinding and taking on more than you should is not sustainable for your health and wellbeing. Nor is it actually helpful to your business or team if you're burned out. Falling into the cycle of burnout is a devastating and sure way to keep you stuck in the million dollar trap.

In this chapter, I'm going to share with you common symptoms of burnout, and the tips that I use to keep myself balanced and happy. This is probably one of the most important chapters in this book because YOU are the heart of your business. If you're burned out, guess what? Nothing in your business can flow or even work efficiently.

So how do you recognize burnout?

If one of your clients calls you, and you look at your phone and you cringe, that's number one. If you're letting calls always go to voicemail, that's another sign. Rejecting opportunities is a huge sign that you need some self-care because you're saying no to potential transactions that could bring you profit.

Another warning sign of burnout is if you're sleeping too much and are reluctant to get out of bed in the morning. If your sleep patterns are changing, ask yourself if you're sleeping to avoid something. My theory is, if you don't get up in the morning like it's Christmas, you're avoiding something. What are you avoiding? Is it the start of production of your day? Maybe you are getting up at the right time, but it's taking you hours to get focused. Why? When you're excited about something that you're working on, you get up, you're driven. You want to take care of it. You're excited about the opportunity. If you're sleeping it off, you're not excited about it.

A more subtle yet clear sign of potential burnout is if you're not innovating or being creative with your business. If you're running on that system you start years ago and haven't implemented anything new, you're running in a circle. This the equivalent of slow, painful death for the entrepreneur. Innovation is how you grow your business. If you have not done anything, then you're just pacifying your daily life.

If no one is referring you to people, then that's a sign. A referral is the cheapest, easiest form of a sale for you. You spend zero money. You only invest your values, you invest in your rapport. Your ROI on a referral is a lot higher than any other marketing efforts that you could put out.

We're humans, not machines, even though we feel like we can work like them. We always say that we don't have the money or time to invest in the rest, relaxation, and emotional release that we deserve. But sometimes we're just taking the money and time that we do have, and either putting 100% of it back into our business or spending it on frivolous things that aren't actually going to help us come back into a state of balance and ease.

I think we have a guard that we put up. It's like a gate. When your gate is shut, you aren't open to other opportunities. You're only open to what your mind is focused on. If you're focused on burnout, then no new ideas are going to come through, because you're in such a negative state of mind.

All the emotions that come with burnout are negative. How can you move to a positive state and build in a positive opportunity-based solution process if you're in burnout? Burnout state can turn things you're passionate about into things you passionately hate. To me, this is the saddest thing.

Somebody said to me the other day, "Oh my gosh, do you ever stop working?" I said, "This isn't work to me." Show me what you think I'm doing every day that's work. This isn't work. I love what I do. It's not work. How could I ever burn out if I don't think that what I do every day is work? I'm passionate about what I do and I love what I do. It's not work. I'm not going to get burnout.

You have to know your limit and your capacity, and not push beyond that. I don't hit those burnout modes anymore because I play within my limits, and it shows. I have more energy to put more time and love into my business, because I'm always making sure that I'm taking care of myself.

All of the screenshots of the haters that I have saved over the years are the people who are most likely in burnout. A hater is what you turn into if you're in burnout. You become angry and volatile. All you want to do is take apart other people. You have no room in your heart or your mind for compassion and forgiveness and acceptance. You get in this mode where you start trolling what everybody else is doing. It's a vicious cycle to have that type of mindset.

You know those times when you've gone to a drive-thru or went into a store or a restaurant of some sort, and you've been in a great mood, and you get to the checkout line or you go to ask a question and somebody is so bitter. They're rude. They roll their eyes or they walk away. These people don't like what they're doing. They live in a negative world. Where they're clocking in is the wrong place for them. I would never want somebody to come to me with a question or an ask for help, and for me to feel so unhappy that I'm just awful to them.

If you find yourself doing that, then you need to step back for a minute and figure out why. Ponder and Journal on these questions:

Why am I so angry?
Why am I so negative?
Why do I have this attitude?
Where is this coming from?
What steps do I need to make to not feel this way?
Where do I need to regroup at?
Where do I need to make changes?

Become aware of your negative thought patterns so that when they come up again, you'll recognize them and can put an end to them.

When you're hustling for a long time and haven't had a moment to breathe, you might find yourself snapping or even exploding. Maybe you even have habits or addictions that poke their head out as band-aid solutions. My best advice is to catch these symptoms before they manifest into a nasty experience, like having a major blowup with a family member or getting physically ill.

Remember that you don't need to get to a state of total burnout to take better care of yourself. Regular rest and relaxation will go a long way in preventing burnout and keeping you in optimal function.

And you don't need to spend tons of money to catch a break!

Tip #1: Take a step back. When you're at work, and you feel yourself getting irritated or frustrated, or like you're on the verge of tears, take a step back. Excuse yourself from the meeting and get some fresh air. Take a brief walk around the block and take some deep breaths. Put your hand on your heart and just connect with yourself for a moment. Maybe you need to pause and reschedule. Maybe you can bring in someone else to take over.

Tip #2: Take a drive and turn up the tunes. My jam is to get in the car and go for an hour ride, listen to '80s music, and sing loud. If I've had a frustrating experience or I'm just overwhelmed, I dance in the car and let my mind be carried by the music. This always relaxes me and puts me in a better mood. Singing and dancing are great ways to relieve stress and prevent burnout. You'll notice that when you come back to work from that place, you'll have more clarity and calmness. Especially when I didn't have a lot of money to stay out of that burnout mode, these therapeutic drives were my go-to.

Tip #3: Take yourself to the spa. Spas are the best. They play great music, cater to your needs, and create an environment where you can put your phone away and be in a beautiful bubble of self-care. Treat yourself to a massage, a facial, mani-pedi, exfoliation, anything your heart desires. I challenge you to spend a whole day at the spa – and to go once a month!

Tip #4: Take a day or weekend trip somewhere, and attend a self-development event. Some people might think, well, if I'm working 24/7 and I'm hustling, why would I go to another event?

I love to go to events that are out of town, because I get the opportunity to be somewhere new, stay at a hotel, relax by the pool and meet amazing new people. All of these things are super energizing and restorative for your soul. I am passionate about growth, and I know that taking that time away helps me grow and business.

If you sign up for a conference, a function, or an event, book yourself a hotel stay one night before, or one night after (or both!). This will help you not only to arrive present and relaxed, but also to integrate your experience and enjoy some extra time to cruise, snooze, be a tourist, or whatever you like.

Tip #5: Take 10% of every sale and invest in yourself. When I started getting a little more money, I would say, you know what? I'm going to take 10% of every sale that I make, and I'm going to invest in something that I want to learn about and am passionate about. Maybe I'm going to treat myself to a concert experience. I'm also going to take myself shopping and make sure I'm looking and feeling my best.

Everybody's ROI is different on a sale, but for me, 10% of $15,000 is a good chunk of money to invest in myself. Even 10% of $5,000 is a good amount of money. If you settle for 1 to 5% and go "invest" in a new toothbrush, is that worth it? Probably not. How are you going to make yourself feel if you invested at least 10% on yourself? For me, investing $1,500 means I can get something really amazing and really meaningful, but at the same time, it's not this huge number that feels irresponsible.

When it comes to shopping, of course, we all feel great with a new outfit or new shoes or a new purse or a new hairdo, new skincare products, anything. Sometimes we find it hard to justify these purchases. For me, I've made it part of my lifestyle to shop, because I enjoy it so much. You can also turn shopping into a powerful way to connect with your business and generate more feelings of appreciation and abundance.

Think about all the things that you see and say, "Oh, I don't have the money for that." You know what? Put it on your list, and make sure that you have applied part of your 10% on every sale on a mini shopping spree. Go buy those nice shoes.

Relive the success of your sale when you shop. Every time you wear those nice shoes, every time you wear that outfit, you're going to remember the transaction that brought you to that outfit or those shoes or that event ticket.

You're going to remember how you felt, and how the person that you worked with felt as well. If you invest in yourself wisely after making a sale, you'll amplify the feelings of accomplishment that you created for yourself and your client. You're reliving it every time that you remember that event, every time you're wearing the outfit and that pair of shoes.

Tip #6: Take 30-45 minutes for personal self-care every single day, right when you wake up and before you go to sleep. Yes, we have children, we have families, we have responsibilities, but if you don't have even an hour for yourself, your priorities are out of whack.

My cup of coffee and my shower is my best time to think about new inventions. I don't want to miss that part of my day, because it kick starts me into showing up for work. Then at the end of the day, I reflect. What did I learn today? If you can't do 30-45 minutes or an hour, do 15 minutes or even five. It's the ritual of saying, "I'm taking care of myself, I'm doing something for me," that's important. That's what feeds your self-esteem and keeps you out of burnout.

If you're a parent, then you're showing up for a lot of people. You have a lot of demands. If you have kids, and you're burnout, you're going to reflect that onto your kids. You're going to be negative. You're not going to have time to play with them or pay attention to them. You're going to think of excuses. You're going to be exhausted. There's going to be a lot of arguments. There's going to be a lot of stress, and it will reflect it and roll through your family and everyone around you.

I read an article that talked about how now that we're all being forced to work on Zoom, women are apologizing for their appearance and how they're showing up. To me, if you don't have time to at least put on your appearance, then that's a big sign you are overwhelmed and stressed out. When you're energized and passionate, you want to appear your best, look your best, and show your best sides.

We've already talked about how your image is your brand. If you're showing up for a Zoom call with a client or a potential client or attending a webinar with unbrushed hair, no makeup on, wearing a tank top or bathrobe or a sundress that makes you look naked, or if you just walked out of the gym, or are taking the call in your car? It's so unprofessional. In my opinion, I think it's disrespectful. If you don't have time to be your best, how do you have time to work on anything?

Your clients want to feel like you respect them. If you don't respect yourself enough to show up as your best, how will they trust that you care about the details of their work? Why would I go to Nordstrom and have a personal shopper that was dressed sloppily? I'd probably go somewhere else.

I'm not saying you have to do hair glam full to the nines every day. It's just showing up every day to be a representative of who you are. If you are a fitness person, then please wear your hat, wear your workout clothes, because that's what you represent, but just don't be sloppy. I'm not in the fitness community so I'm going to show up in business attire. It doesn't have to be necessarily a dress, but it's going to be nice. My hair is going to be brushed and it's going to be fixed. I'm going to have a little bit of makeup on. I don't have to come out like I'm walking into the gala, but I need to have something on so I don't look like I just rolled out of bed. It's not fashion. it's a feeling.

With Zoom, there's this culture of, "Oh, I've got sweatpants on, but I have a nice shirt on. Nobody will know I'm in my sweats." I'm sorry, but if half of my body feels like it's comfy and the other doesn't, I'm confusing myself. What am I doing? Am I in bed? Half of my body is in bed and half of it is at work. No, it's not. It's all at work, or none of it is.

You're a successful, thriving businessperson. Be you. Put some earrings and put your ring on. Put your necklace on, just as if you were walking out the door because you know what? You are. You're leaving your cozy cave and showing up to do business. If this feels tiring, if this feels like a stretch, if you just don't have the energy or enthusiasm to show up, you might be in burnout mode.

Is it okay to experience stress now and then? Sure. But "hustle" culture normalizes stress. Being stressed out regularly is what happens when you're in the million dollar trap. Stress can do numbers. Stress can cause heart attacks and strokes. It can make your hair fall out. It can change your joints, your muscles. Stress can even kill you. Your mind can't grow if it's stressed.

I've seen what happens when people are addicted to the hustle, get stressed, and become burned out.

Sometimes this happens: you partner with someone you work with daily. It can start to go downhill when, for instance, you feel you are doing most of the work alone. You may be missing time with the family, or "you" time.

You can get to the point of no return. You can't do it anymore. You are drained, stressed, and have lost your passion.

Take a minute right now if you are feeling this way currently. Take a deep breath.

Change needs to happen immediately. You are good at what you do, but you are allowing someone else to steal your passion, your life, your goals. Stop taking on an unhealthy portion of the workload alone. Remove yourself from the situation and you will have a huge weight off your shoulders. You will skyrocket.

Now watch your life change so much from being financially distraught, feeling empty, hitting your head against the wall to now spending time doing what you love and having time back with your family and friends.

It's so important to me to raise the people I work with and to be an inspiration for all women especially to find balance in their lives. I believe that if more women took care of themselves and got out of burnout, that we would naturally be more compassionate and supportive of one another.

I also believe that your business is a powerful vehicle to uplift other people and to help them transform their stress and burnout. When you model what it looks like to not live with constant stress, to not be burned out, you can create an environment with a lot more productivity and innovation, less complaining and hating on others.

If you've come this far with me on the journey to creating a business lifestyle that truly fulfills your passion, all you want to do is share and build everybody else around you.

Currently, I'm in Orange Beach, Alabama. It's beautiful. It's sunny. And I'm not just at the beach. I'm at the beach with 12 other tribe members from our business. You know why? Because they earned it. They worked their butts off, and I don't want them in burnout mode.

Not only am I going to reward them and get them out of burnout mode, we're going to spend time together. We're going to build a bigger bond together on this trip. We're going to cook together. We're going to laugh together. We're going to cheer together. We're going to lay out in the sun together. I mean, just the memories alone are worth the investment.

This is the new prosperity. This is the new abundance. It's beyond the hustle. It's sharing it with other people. It would be so lonely to share abundance with yourself. Right? Share it with other people.

I mean, do you want somebody to read your eulogy and say, "Oh, that was a wicked bitch?" Hell no. How about, "Tracy,

CHAPTER 5:: FROM BURNOUT TO BEACH MODE

she was supportive. She helped me. She inspired me." That's what you want. When I'm 80 years old in my Cracker Barrel chair on my front porch, I just want to go through a long list of people that I was able to impact. I want to remember all the amazing times I had with my family, my team, with my clients, and with and for my community.

You deserve that same experience.

Get out of burnout. Get to the beach. Jump in your car, and just go. Leave the million dollar trap behind, and never look back!

CHAPTER 6:

UPLEVEL YOUR INNER CIRCLE

In this chapter, I'm going to share with you the wisdom I've gained about choosing your inner circle wisely. Having a high-level inner circle is a critical key to escaping the million dollar hustle, and growing to the next level of your potential in business and in life. The people in your inner circle are a mirror reflection of who you are on the inside, and the choices you're making.

When I say "high level," I'm not necessarily just talking about people who are successful on paper or who are big-shot CEOs. I'm talking about people who have a high quality of thoughts, attitudes, and energy. People who are mindful, warm, supportive, good listeners, and who can engage with you on a deeper level than just swapping statuses and going shopping.

When you were a teenager, you might have had a group of friends that you did everything with. The things they said, the places they went, and the clothes they wore all influenced you and your choices. Or maybe you grew up mostly surrounded by your family, your siblings and parents or guardians, and took on a lot of their habits and choices. We all grow up in different environments with different social situations. Some of us have experienced being ostracized, bullied, abused, or betrayed, and that can make it difficult for us to know who to trust, open up to, and let into our inner circle – even though we're "grownups" now.

Even though we come from different pasts, we all share the same desire to have a supportive circle of family and friends around us. Having a close inner circle is not only part of human nature, but it's necessary for any leader or business owner to thrive.

We are shaped so much by our environments and the people around us. Do you remember having a teacher at school who left an impact on you? Maybe they believed in you when no one else did? Have you worked with a mentor who helped you shine? Do you have memories of childhood friends who taught you new things about life?

In the earlier chapters of this book, I shared with you how my childhood was full of people talking down to me and telling me I wouldn't amount to anything. It took me going through a lot of struggle and heartache to realize that I was worth more than what anybody thought of me.

When I was in my young adult years, I look back now and realize I was spending a lot of my time hanging out at bars with people who were drinking and complaining. These attitudes reflected my own. I had a lot of negativity from past experiences and I was mindlessly living the same habits and choices that kept me stuck in crappy cycles and experiences.

These days, my inner circle is populated with a handful of ambitious, open-minded, and focused people who I know I can call on for any reason, at literally any time. I've learned that this is because I've chosen to follow my passion, my purpose, and what lights me up.

I want you to think of the top five people you're currently hanging out with or chatting with the most. What kinds of attitudes and energies do they bring to your interactions? Do they fill up your time sharing stories of their failures and disappointments? Are they constantly nitpicking at you or giving you unsolicited advice? Are they good people who mean well, but who get cautious or distant when it comes to talking about next-level dreams and visions?

Up leveling your inner circle starts with getting super clear and honest about your current relationships. Do you keep certain people around just because they have something you want? Do you find yourself going out of your way to "be there" for people who "need you," under the masquerade of friendship? At this level of your career and your influence, you need to put a hard stop to any relationships that are not mirroring back your greatest qualities.

The kind of relationship you want to cultivate is with other leaders; people like you who have vision, depth, and passion. The friends and family you choose are not here to sugarcoat everything and treat you like a princess 24/7. They will hold you accountable to your word and call you out on your bullshit. They will also be able to share their wisdom with you from a genuine place of love and care for your success.

When I woke up and realized that my drinking friends were just holding me back, I made the quick decision to level-up my circle. That decision came from a desire to be a better leader, a better parent, and a better person. I knew that I owed it to myself, to my family, and to my business to show up with more integrity. I didn't want to carry the weight of having stressful, even unhealthy relationships on me. Because it was showing in my performance, it was showing in my brand, and it was showing on my self-esteem.

Looking back now at that time, around the beginning of my business journey, I see that I was a totally different person. Sometimes I can't believe that people even hired me! I wasn't showing up 100% where I needed to. I was losing business often, and I didn't realize it was because of the impression people were getting about me when they would see me out and about, or see me on social media. I was so wrapped up in my own little world that I didn't pay attention to how I was putting myself out there and who I was attracting – or repelling.

Who you socialize with not only directly influences your inner being, it also directly reflects on your brand, which directly affects your value and how people in your market perceive you. One social media post can go a long way to destroying your credibility and reputation. Deleting old posts from your party years is just the starting point. You have to be living and sharing the real values that you believe in. That's what's going to build your brand, and what's also going to call in the right people who resonate with your message.

Whether you realize it or not, word gets around about the people you're hanging out with. Especially if you're already at a level of prominence and people know who you are – there could be photos or tweets or texts circulating about who's elbows you're rubbing at an event. Somebody's going to post something about you being somewhere, and that's going to reflect on your brand.

This isn't to say that we have to monitor every single social media post in our network. What this is really about is understanding that who you are around reflects who you are. And, ultimately, you always have a choice around who you interact with, what parties you go to, what shops you frequent, and who you follow on social media.

You need to decide that you are too valuable to waste your time with people who are going to bring you down. And then you need to stick to that decision, setting clear boundaries and using the word "No" with confidence.

I used to hang out with people who were living life lower than the average. They couldn't be supportive of me, because they wanted me not to persevere and have a different life. Because how would that make them look and feel?

Now, my goal is to be the "dumbest" person in the room. I want to be around intelligent, wise, experienced, and interesting people whose knowledge I can soak up like a sponge.

If people don't want you to be successful or can't support you, then that's just not your right tribe. You've got to make the invitation to your inner circle exclusive, and high-ticket.

Raise your standards, and then raise them again. There's no grey area when it comes to determining if someone is good for you or not. You can feel it in your gut, you can feel it when you're around them. You can see it and hear it in the way other people relate to them, too. Heed those warning signs and red flags and don't make excuses for anybody.

In theory, deciding to surround yourself with supportive, rock-solid people is easy, but putting it into practice can be difficult.

Just like you have sleeping patterns, you have social patterns. Your body gets used to this pattern and this everyday life. For me, it was a struggle to get real with it and say, "You know what? I'm in a habit of who I see when I go out." I'm at the bar at 6 pm out of habit. I'm texting with this person out of habit. I'm in this relationship out of habit.

You might feel awkward, or face conflict when you start to ignore those calls or messages and decline certain social invitations. Sometimes you have to put on your power heels and have really difficult conversations, to "break up" with friends, teammates, even romantic partners who you know are not a match for you.

There's also this FOMO, or "Fear of Missing Out," that can haunt us when we start distancing ourselves from our usual social circle. I like to replace this with JOMO, the "Joy of Missing Out." There are so many more amazing, nourishing, life-giving things we can be doing with our time that will all improve our business.

Ask yourself, what's more important to you than that hangout or that gossip sesh?

Your vision, maybe?

Your kids?

That hobby you've always wanted to put time and energy into?

Getting extra rest and hours of self-care?

Time in nature?

The list is endless.

Start making a list of all the things you could do with the time and energy you'll free up without those negative relationships.

For me, when I realized what was on the other side of the things I was "missing," I never looked back. The people I needed to cancel from my life traveled in a pack, which made it easier for me to walk away. I did cold-turkey style, and I recommend this way as well.

Even if you have a long-standing arrangement with someone like you've paid them/agreed to it/scheduled it in advance, cancel. This goes for mentors or coaches that you've outgrown or who you feel don't actually have your best interest at heart. Cancel, cancel, cancel. At this level, we are only saying YES from our soul to the people and places who light us up, fully.

The beautiful thing about cutting people out is that you're not only helping yourself – you're actually liberating them to find the people who are more aligned with them and their journey. How great is that? It's a total win-win. When I stopped hanging out with draining social circles, I was like, "Oh my gosh, I can't believe I put myself in the cycle in the first place." You'll experience the same thing, and just watch how it changes your life.

Once you start cutting people out, you'll see very quickly who's on your side and who's not, who your real family is, and who your friends are. There's this misconception that when you leave your social circle, your life is going to be boring and that you're not going to have any friends. But when you start to validate your own worth, you'll attract more amazing friends in your life. I couldn't ask for better friends and the relationships that I have now. The networks that I have, the people I've met along this new journey are just real. They're at the same level as I am. They understand, they can support me, they can have the conversations to help me in areas that I need it, or can offer new ideas, and that's huge.

Movies and media often portray successful rich people as greedy, but I find that the more successful you are, the more you want to give, the more you want to help others. People at a high level of success are turned on by sharing and networking. They love connecting with other people who help them grow. They want to share their bright ideas and they want to meet other people who can relate to them. Starting to mingle at this level is a powerful, amazing feeling.

Because I believe so strongly in the power of finding your tribe, I've started a Facebook community for women to elevate and empower other women. I coach women 1:1, and a huge part of my coaching revolves around the idea that we have to up-level and support one another as women in business. When you're the only entrepreneur in your group of friends, it can be lonely. You might feel like you can connect with other business owners on a superficial level, but can't imagine them ever being your friends. Sounds too good to be true, right? The thing is, you don't have to be stuck in the belief that the friends you have now are the only ones you deserve. The people you want to meet are out there, and connecting with them is all about declaring that you deserve the best of the best.

I never understood what real friends were until I got over that belief that I was stuck with the people and the circumstances I grew up with. The younger me could have never imagined that I could pick up the phone and call anybody in my circle, and they would be there for me in any way they could. Today, that is my reality. When you believe it is out there for you, it can come in. This is a universal law.

When it comes to the million dollar trap, the key to remember here is that your inner circle is going to either keep you at the level of financial success you're at or assist you in breaking your limits and going beyond to the next level. You want to be around people who see abundance everywhere.

People who are stuck financially will reflect where you are stuck. People who are constantly generating new income and innovating their business are going to inspire the money maker in you. And it all comes down to mindset.

We either have a scarcity mindset, where there's not enough for everybody, we have to hustle to make it, and we have to compete to win. This is the opposite mindset to the flow of trusting the universe, knowing that there is absolutely enough money for everybody, and staying in your lane to allow your greatest potential to flourish.

The more clear you get on your message and who you truly are, the more it's going to attract people who are also at that same vibration. I love to learn and I love to grow. I'm attracted to people who are learners and growers. I like being focused and creative. I attract people who are focused and creative. My work comes from a desire to be of service to my community, and I attract those who are also serving their communities in their unique way.

Time and space don't matter when it comes to building those relationships. My friends don't live close to me. They're not in my immediate community in Atlanta. Andréa, the woman who published this book, lives across the country, yet I know that she is a trusted part of my inner circle. She understands me, supports me, inspires me, and shares her energy of abundance, prosperity, and self-confidence with the world. My inner circle is not necessarily people that I talk to every day, but they are the ones who know that we are both just a phone call away from anything the other needs.

So how do you actually meet these amazing people who deserve to be a part of your inner circle? The trick is to be in alignment with yourself and follow your intuition when it comes to networking. When you feel sparked by curiosity to attend an event that promises like-minded people, go. When you get introduced or referred to a potential client or partner with whom you feel a real resonance, explore that. When you find yourself at the coffee shop making small talk with someone and quickly realizing you have lots in common, swap numbers. If you're drawn to work with a mentor or bring on a coach, they could also become part of your inner circle. The people in your mentor or coach's network could potentially become some of your best friends. Who knows? Go beyond your community, go beyond your industry. Attend new conferences, meetups, masterminds, and experiences that can offer you a fresh pool of perspectives and personalities to play with.

Meeting your inner circle is all about being open and trusting that the right people will come into your life at the right time. The only work you have to do is to cut out those toxic relationships and never look back. Because once you've weeded your garden, the flowers can grow. The following exercises can help you apply what you're learning.

Exercise #1: Write down an inventory list of all the qualities you like in your friends, i.e. supportive, open-minded, honest...

Then, circle the qualities on that list that YOU bring to relationships.

The next time you have an opportunity to, practice bringing out those qualities in yourself. This will help you recognize them in other people.

Exercise #2: Set the intention to find an event you'd like to go to or a group you'd like to join. For example, a mastermind, a summit, a conference, a retreat, where you know other like-minded people will be there.

When it comes up, clear your schedule and book that ticket!

Exercise #3: Reach out to someone you admire on social media or want to strike up a friendship with. Make a date to take them out for coffee and get to know them. Sometimes, you have to make the first move!

CHAPTER 7:

QUIT YOURSELF

You've followed all the steps that will get you out of the million dollar trap. You have a robust team, are clear on your brand, and are practicing the art of delegation. Business is running and money is coming into the bank. But you might be thinking, "Tracy, there's a problem here. I'm realizing that I hate what I am doing!" What if you've reached a great level of success, but you're not feeling stoked about your business? This chapter is all about recognizing when you need to reassess if your business is in alignment with your vision and your dream for yourself.

What's important to realize, first of all, is that the businesses you choose to create should always be a vehicle for you to serve others with your passion. When it's my time to leave this Earth, I don't just want people to think of me and say, "Oh, she sold a lot of houses." I want my legacy to be that I made a difference in people's lives. And I do. I make a difference in a lot of buyers' and sellers' lives every single day, and I am also committed to helping our team members create different lifestyles for themselves.

Beyond the people I directly serve at work, there's also the community where I live and online, where I can reach people who want to grow a business or who are stuck.

Ask yourself: Do I genuinely care about the people I'm serving? Do I wake up every day excited about what I can create? Do I feel nourished by the success stories of my clients and my team? Do I go to bed at night feeling grateful and inspired by the progress I've made? If the answer to any of these questions is "No," or "Not really," then I want to invite you to take the time to feel into why you're still running the business you're in.

We live in a world of endless possibilities, and I know for a fact that you are never limited to just one career path or way of doing business. I believe that everybody should find their passion, everybody should find their purpose, and everybody should live the life that they can create from that. In my world, this energy is what keeps attracting more and more opportunities to me. People can see that I am the real deal. I'm not faking it. When you love what you do, your passion will carry out into every circle you touch, and it will be magnetic, powerful, and attractive.

So again, if you've reached a certain level of success in your business but you're not feeling passionate about it, you need to quit yourself. Quit the "you" that is wearing a mask. Quit the "you" that is following a prescribed pattern for your life and career. Quit the "you" that is trying to make it work on the inside when it's not working at all! You need to quit lying to yourself and telling yourself that you're happy and satisfied. You need to quit your habits of saying yes when

CHAPTER 7 :: QUIT YOURSELF

you mean no. You need to quit the you that is not living your truth. It's time for you to do what you want to do.

Do you see people who are making this mistake? They have built a business or they're making money, but they're not happy. It's obvious when you're not passionate about something because it affects your entire business – especially your client experience.

We can feel people through their body language and tonality. So you know if somebody is passionate about what they're doing. Many times, when I'm out shopping, even in the Starbucks drive-thru, I'll encounter a person who looks glum or even downright pissed off. When this happens, I'll look at my children and I'll say, "Oh, they don't like their jobs." They're not interested in me or how I'm doing or how they can genuinely help me. They're not spreading their love and good energy in making their world a better place.

If I have that experience with a company, why would I want to go back? At the core of it all, if you, yourself, aren't feeling jazzed about showing up to work, and you're hiring people who are following that same pattern, the impression you're giving the world is that your company is not a fun place to be or a good-feeling place to do business. You're only going to experience real success in a position that you are passionate about because it will always be a joyful one.

Another important reason to be aligned with your passion is that if you're passionate about what you're doing, no outer circumstances can stop you from achieving what you set out to do. By contrast, when you're not aligned with your passion, problems and roadblocks happen constantly.

As I write this, we are in a global pandemic. The average person might think about the real estate business and say, "That's going to shit. No one's buying or selling right now." You know what? At the peak of the pandemic, I sold 18 houses in a week and a half. We closed almost 100 more homes than the year prior. It was just crazy.

The reason we accomplished that was because of the passion that drove us to become flexible, adaptable, and create solutions where other people might see problems.

Knowing that this would technically be the third recession in my professional life, I was prepared.

During the first recession, I didn't feel the effects as much. During the second one, I lost everything. I knew I never wanted to go through that or put my family through that ever again.

Because of that, I keep myself aware and informed about how to stay on the leading edge of my industry, so that I can always provide service and value, no matter how our brick-and-mortar offices are affected.

When 2020 rolled around, we were already in a position of being prepared for anything, because we need to show up for our community. With people being quarantined in their houses, and social distancing, all of that put a damper on the excitement of being able to go and look at homes.

Our question was, how were we going to get clients inside the spaces they wanted to see? Right away we moved to offering different types of videos and virtual walkthroughs, as well as virtual appointments. Because my passion keeps me on top of the game, we had already invested in the technology in order to support people in the virtual shift. We didn't know it was going to occur this quickly, but people who saw ahead and into the future with digital marketing, online relationships, virtual networking, were ahead of all of the curve.

When you show up, and others don't, it's very noticeable. When all these other companies are going out of business and are afraid, what I'm experiencing is a level of success that is so natural and effortless.

In an earlier chapter, I told you that I'm always looking out for the endgame of my clients. When new roadblocks or circumstances pop up, my team is able to assess them and say, "Wow, I guess we didn't look at it that way. But this has made us look at it. And this is a good idea. Let's do this. And it works."

Being focused on the endgame comes from having passion and wanting to show up. Having passion allows you to become flexible and adaptable.

For example, we examined the need for brochures for a house. Was that necessary? No, everything is online. Why were we still doing paper in front of a house? Nobody drops by anymore! We were only doing it because it was old school. We were appeasing the process.

When we switched to virtual, we started saving a lot of money by just transitioning our services online.

And what's more – these transactions are multimillion dollar hauls. Because I love what I do, I've been able to position myself where my passion and innovation are attracting the luxury buyer, who could buy from anyone.

I also know that I can't create everything myself, and I need to have the right team and support to move quickly and create quickly. So, across the board from a video team, to a design team, to executive staff, we have to make sure that everybody is on board, able to adapt to changing circumstances and keep going towards the endgame. This is what people look for in a leader – this decision-making ability, this passion, and this commitment. If you aren't showing up in this way, then you'll never inspire people to follow you.

This leads us to another indicator that you need to quit yourself – when you are constantly overstepping your commitments to take on too much. We've already talked about the importance of hiring, firing, and delegating well. The other piece to this is only doing what no one else but you can do.

Knowing what you do that drives the best forward and your best use and abilities for faster growth is the box you show up in every day. This doesn't mean you don't check on the other boxes that you have delegated – do not be a micromanager. Always be working on what you work on the best.

When you create your org chart, make sure that you stay in the areas of growth that you committed to, and stay out of the ones that you didn't put yourself in. It can be so hard when you're starting your business because you think you have to wear all the hats. That mentality will keep you stuck, because you have to be able to release the hat to someone else in order to grow past the seven-figure mark and thrive.

Sometimes, staying in your growth lane means even turning over the running of your company to someone else entirely. If you're in a position right now where you want to make a big change in your business, perhaps even free yourself from it entirely to pivot and do more of what you love, maybe hiring a CEO is your next step. Part of quitting yourself is realizing that you can't do it all, and that's okay. We're often told to keep "stepping up" in our lives to make things happen. But everything, every role, and business has its season, and you've got to be able to step back just as much as you step up. You have to be able to stop and say, "I quit everything."

Now what do you do if you're running a company that you want to quit, but you don't want the company itself to dissolve? You have to look at the entire operation of your company, and ask, What are the things that drive the company? What do I need to do to set up a new leader to take on that which I can't anymore? Get clear on what knowledge and insight you need to package and pass on. Enlist your closest team members to assist you in preparing for the transition. Believing that "I'm the only one who can do it," will keep you stuck and unhappy forever.

My dream for you is that you quit holding yourself back from the greatest success you can create in the world. Quit your ego, quit the beliefs that keep you trapped. Always remember that when your endgame is showing up in passionate service, you will be able to navigate any challenges that come your way.

CHAPTER 8:
THE GROWTH ZONE

One of the most beautiful and awesome things about being a visionary and a leader is that you're always being given opportunities to expand your mind. Our last chapter was about quitting yourself if you're not aligned with your passion.

Now, when you're past the million-dollar hustle and feel truly aligned with your passion, you have space to continue to stretch and grow. In this chapter, we're going to be talking about the importance of combining your passion with flexibility and adaptability, so that you can continue to grow and scale yourself beyond one business.

When people ask me, "Tracy, how do you do it all? How do you keep moving and growing and evolving?" First, I say that my mind is crazy and it doesn't rest, and it's always trying to think outside of the current project. I just have fun thinking up new ideas.

So I am always balancing between staying focused on what I'm doing and going into creative visionary mode. I don't stop myself from having fun, I allow myself to explore and expand. That's a big key for me and why I'm so happy every day, even when the work is tough.

Some say that multitasking is not good, or it's not a thing, but it's definitely a thing. Here I am today, shooting TV shows, writing this book, and getting interviews, all the while running my businesses. I'm not trapped in the cycle of the mundane.

My life is an example of what it looks like to continue to stretch and grow, and the world is showing up to say, "Yes. If you want this, you can have it."

I remember back when I was stuck in old mindsets, I had so much time on my hands and I was often bored. Now I always say, "Gosh, I wish I had a lot of that time back!" I'm only half-joking, because I've got so much going on now, and I wonder how I was ever bored. Once you learn your passion and understand your worth, you can't ever imagine being bored. There are so many ways to expand and grow. As much as I loved my first business, I couldn't imagine doing the same thing forever. That's why I've continued to stretch myself and create new businesses, my clothing store and coaching practice, which serve different parts of my being and allow me to help more people.

What I've learned from becoming a business mogul is that someone who can manage one multimillion dollar company can manage five. When you've figured out how to do it, it's just about applying the same systems and strategies to multiple industries. You can take the process from one company to the next, and tweak it on that particular brand and company. For the most part, the outline is the same. It's a formula, it's a pattern. When you start to become a mogul, running multiple businesses and multiple industries, you have to continue to look at the pattern of, "Okay, where am I hustling at this level? Where am I falling into the trap? How can I keep growing and keep expanding?"

Again, it's about stepping into this zone of finding the right people that can go into positions that not only lead and grow the company with you but take on certain roles that you don't have to be a part of. You absolutely can create a company that you don't even need to be a part of. For me, it was amazing to see this in action with my store, Southern Lace Boutique. I didn't have to have full control of it, I knew that it could run by itself once I had the right processes in place and trained my team correctly. They needed to understand every aspect of the vision, which came down to my saying, "If you do this, it's not going to work and if you do this, this is going to work." That kind of high-level structure and instruction helps to keep the processes at play. That being said, I never create something and then leave it to become stagnant. I am always checking in and continuing to innovate and adapt with my team.

So, if you have a passion for something, you can create it. Maybe you don't have to be the person who has to be there every single day, as long as you find the right person that sees your vision, that understands your vision, and who is going to take full responsibility to run the business as if it were you. The reason you'll be able to do this is because you've created this valuable brand, which is you. You are going to be attracting other business-minded people who want to grow their own brand. When you can create an opportunity for those people to align with your brand and support your business as leaders, your brand becomes an asset that attracts more and more opportunities for your business to grow.

I was talking to a friend of mine who has a clothing store and her brand is for a certain type of clientele. However, she had the opposite clientele running her store, so the alignment didn't make sense. When I walked in, I'm like, "Well this doesn't look like alignment. Your customer has got to be confused." My friend was on the cover of fitness magazines and presenting a certain brand. But the image that I got when I walked into the store was completely day and night different. Consistency and reliability in the communication of your brand are what will allow you to create a business that you can hand over in trust that it will continue to grow without your constant supervision.

Being creative and letting yourself stretch your mind with new ideas is one part of the growth zone. The other part is knowing how to be logical, clear, and black and white when it comes to handling challenges.

It's not like everything is rah, rah, rah, some huge pompom show. There might be shit shows. Just because you're in the growth zone doesn't mean that you're not going to get these obstacles flying at you from left and right. But the most important thing is you don't fall out of the growth zone, you keep growing, you keep optimizing and you handle whatever comes your way.

Problems will come, but they all boomerang back out too, so it's all on how you deal with it. The more successful you are, the more boomerangs may hit you. The more that you have the shit shows, the more that you learn how to deal with them in a clear way. You learn how to tell it like it is. I've often heard myself say, "If they don't like it, I'm sorry, but this is the way it's going to be." Lots of people try to sugarcoat things and avoid direct communication. This backs everything up and causes lots of problems with trust and reliability. It's impossible to grow when you sugarcoat stuff. I've learned to just ask for the facts so that I can journey quickly to the solution to any problem. The fastest way to get there is always communication.

    I feel that so few women are really making it to the growth zone, because we sugarcoat our communication and our leadership. We wear our hearts on our sleeves, and I'm not saying not to wear your heart on your sleeve, but to recognize that in certain situations, it's not the most effective way of dealing with what's in front of you. I think we take a lot of things personally, and if we can separate what is personal from what is business, recognize the difference, we'll have a lot more energy to find solutions and keep growing. We are here to exemplify and not only teach the growth zone, but live the growth zone and be a real-world example of it.

    Like I said earlier, I used to take personal attacks a lot, and sometimes I still do. I'm still learning through it. But it's not as often anymore that a personal attack can put me down for a long time. They used to burn me out, and then I wouldn't grow, and things would fall through the cracks. I learned that if I took the personal attacks without getting emotionally invested, I could use the experience to make myself more powerful, to produce more, to show up in a bigger way. I realized that sometimes people have bad days and I was just their point of contact for their bad day.

The growth zone reflects a level of maturity and wisdom that comes naturally when you've lived through the challenges of business leadership and let yourself learn from them.

Throughout this whole book, we've talked about the different mindsets and aspects that can keep you trapped in the million dollar hustle. I want to encourage you to keep identifying where you're burning out, keep creating an environment full of people who are aligned with your vision, keep embodying your brand and message, and stay driven by a passion for something greater than dollars in the bank.

Before we move on to the completion of this journey, I want to leave you with a few journal prompts that you can use to reflect on as you get familiar with the growth zone in your own life:

- Where do I currently feel stuck in my thinking or my business?
- If I could create another business, what would it be?
- What does my best day look like?
- What kind of people are going to stretch my mind?
- How can I surround myself with those people?

CHAPTER 9:

CELEBRATE

I remember being a kid when I couldn't wait for the Sears catalog or the J.C. Penney catalog to show up at our house. I would make paper dolls out of it.

As I was cutting out the outfits, I would think, "Wow, look at all these outfits, look at all these shoes, look at all of this stuff."

Once you get past that million dollar hustle mindset, life becomes like opening that Sears catalog. It's never-ending. It's hundreds and hundreds of pages of opportunity. You'll have people wanting you to be onstage. People want you on webinars. They want you on their podcast. They want you as part of their blogs, or as their coach, or their agent. Whatever your passion is, they're going to search for you. They're going to find you.

Once you've made seven figures, you've proven you're smart. You've proven you've got a good work ethic. You've proven that you're able to take a vision and make it real. What makes you extraordinary is that you're also rooted in your passion; you're happy and alive and vibrant. This energy is what creates the magic in your life, that inspires new creative ideas, and helps you skyrocket the seeds you've planted beyond the million dollar mark.

Whether you believe in things like the law of attraction or not, you can't deny that people who have joy and happiness in their life seem to be "lucky." They seem to have things happen for them.

The truth is, we all have the power to create our own path. When you open yourself up to share your passion, and people find you, you realize there were opportunities out there that you just couldn't see until you changed the way that you were doing life.

Your thinking shapes the world that you live in, and when you commit to a mindset of abundance and success, the right people and opportunities can find you anywhere you are.

I'm often asking myself how I can touch more lives. I'm always expanding my mind and opening up that catalog of more opportunities. I've learned that just when you think you've seen everything life has to offer, another level of opportunity appears. What will you follow? What will you choose? How strongly will you let your passion guide you?

When I was little, I lived through Barbies. To me, Barbie was the hardest working woman ever; she had more careers than anybody. She had every color of stiletto. You could see endless opportunities for Barbie in the toy store, stacked in a row on the shelf – from artist to rock star to firefighter and scientist. Barbie had mansions and vacation homes, pets, and best friends.

I thought I was just playing back then, but I was directing my own life at a young age. I lived a fantasy through Barbie that I'm experiencing now.

Your childhood dreams are valid, they're sacred, they're special. My hope is that you'll apply everything you've learned in this book so that you can be living your dreams too.

I see a world where all of us are stepping up into genuine leadership, creating the businesses that we know the world needs, and bringing a new level of care, compassion, clarity, and impact to our communities.

I see women business leaders getting tired of the grind and going all-in on their passion.

If you've stuck with me all the way to the end of this book, I see you – and I know it's just the beginning of our journey together!

For me, waking up every day knowing that I've broken out of the million dollar trap feels amazing. I used to feel so worn out, and now I know there are no limits to what I can create. I have a big smile on my face. I've released all of the negative energy in my life, all the non-supportive relationships. All the processes and policies and procedures that weren't working are history.

Now I have a clean slate of positivity, like a new mindset, a new wardrobe.

Every day, you get to choose how you show up for your life. You are unstoppable, and you've got this. Celebrate yourself! There's no end zone, there's no U-turn, it's just go.

Big high five to you, sister. Now you can truly create your greatest dreams, your wildest success, because you have released all of the energy that would have kept you stuck in place for so long.

You rock those stilettos! Go make the world a better place today.

Made in the USA
Columbia, SC
02 April 2021